ORDINARY, EXTRAORDINARY

ORDINARY, EXTRAORDINARY

MY FATHER'S LIFE

Bernard Pinsky

Excerpts from *The Tailor Project: How 2,500 Holocaust Survivors Found a New Life in Canada*, by Andrea Knight, Paula Draper, and Nicole Bryck (Toronto: Second Story Press, 2020), published with permission of Second Story Press (secondstorypress.ca).

First edition published in 2023

ISBN 978-1-7390226-2-4

Cover and interior design: Alex Hennig (alexhennig.ca)
Copy editing: Dallas Harrison

behind the BOOK

Produced by Behind the Book
behindthebook.ca

Printed and bound with KDP

Front cover photo: *Rubin Pinsky, circa 1949.*
Back cover photo: From left: *Rubin, Harry, and Chasia, 1947.*

This book is dedicated to Holocaust survivors and their families, whatever became of them in their postwar lives.

Contents

PART I

Ordinary, Extraordinary: My Father's Life

I wrote this book and presented it to my father, Rubin Pinsky, on his 72nd birthday, December 5, 1996. What a crazy idea for a birthday present! By that time, his body and mind showed the effects of wear and tear. I doubt that he ever read the book through; maybe he thumbed through it. Reading a book in English was beyond him by then, and he had never been much of a whole book reader anyway. In 2022–23, I added to and edited that 1996 version to provide information about his final years that was not in the original. During both the first writing and the recent changes, this was a work of love and a humbling experience; how easy my life has been compared with his. I remain grateful to him and to other Holocaust survivors for coming back to life and making my and other future generations' lives possible.

Virtually everything that I've written until the time that my father arrived in Winnipeg I found out directly or indirectly from him; sometimes I had to drag it out of him because he was reluctant to talk about some of what happened. I had some information and corroboration from his brother, Harry, and his sister Chasia and from a film made by a group of Israelis in the early 1990s about Gzetl because it was also their hometown. My father was also interviewed on videotape by the local Holocaust Education Society about his experiences in the Second World War, once in 1983 and again about 1990; in watching those videotapes, I learned for the first time many of the details described in this account. Most of the details he would not disclose except when a video record was to be made and preserved for future generations. When I was young, my father would lie by our beds and tell me and my brother Max some of his adventures in the forests as our nightly bedtime story. I wanted to hear time and time again about how he fought a wolf for food and how for years he lived only on what the forest offered. It seemed like a tale of a legendary hero, and it didn't seem to be possible that it had involved my own dad. He didn't tell me about killing people, or blowing up trains, or cutting telephone or electricity wires. Was that deliberate? Perhaps he was saving my young ears from hearing about violence. Those bedtime stories were told to me in the late 1950s and early 1960s, so he would have been well ahead of his time if he was concerned about exposing children to stories of violence. More likely he was saving himself from the agony of having to think about that difficult time again. My father was always sensitive about it. For example, he broke down crying while speaking to an audience of high school students in 1992 at the annual Holocaust symposium held at the University of British Columbia. His task was to describe his experiences in the Holocaust. In the middle of his explanation, 50 years after the events, he stopped speaking and wept. He was suddenly short of breath and almost collapsed. He was taken from the room. After he rested for a while, it was determined that there was nothing physically wrong with him. He was simply overwhelmed by emotion. Despite these difficulties, and how much it affected him mentally and physically, my father continued to speak publicly about the Holocaust to hundreds of high school students every year at the Holocaust symposium until he was no longer able to do so.

—Bernard Pinsky

CHAPTER 1

Gzetl

My father was born in a town called Gzetl, about 100 kilometres north of Pinsk in the area currently an independent state known as Belarus. Yet, in all his years in Canada, he never wanted to go back to Gzetl, his birthplace. He didn't want to see the town where he was born, to wander the streets where he played as a child, to see the burned remains of the house in which he had spent his first 15 years, had embraced his mother, had learned from his father. I can't say that I blame him after what happened. What is amazing to me is that so many people who went through the same or similar experiences as my father did do want to go back to see their birthplaces, explore their roots, and be immersed in their previous lives. But experiencing and surviving the Holocaust affected everyone differently. It made some mad, others chronically inconsolable, some feeling that the world owes them a decent life, and others became as strong as steel. It affected my father in many ways, but he was one of the lucky ones. He found or, better yet, created for himself a normal, healthy life, with the help of others and with the wisdom and the luck of choosing a great country in which to spend his life after coming so close to death. We have all seen some who could not revive their souls after being drowned in torment and despair. Happily, my father was not one of them.

The town was called Gzetl in Yiddish, and those who spoke no Yiddish, the masters of the town, even though the majority of the population was Jewish, had other names for it. The area of Belarus was constantly being overrun by one power or another since it was located vulnerably at the beginning of the great central plains that sweep far into Russia to the east and into Poland to the west. The Belarusians were used to paying homage to another power, usually either Polish or Russian, but it mattered not to the Jews, or most of the other Belarusians for that matter, who made up the police of the town or to whom taxes were paid. Russians and Poles treated Belarusians with equal disdain, taking what they could for their central government, or for themselves (legally of course), but knowing that the pickings were slim. The Belarusians, for the most part, were subsistence farmers, the Jews were craftsmen or small merchants, and relations in general between the rulers and the ruled were civil if not friendly. After the Great War, everyone knew their place, and there wasn't much trouble. Until the 1930s of course. But we will come to that later.

When the Poles were in control, the town was officially called Zdzieciol. When the Russians ruled, the town was called Gatlobo. Today it is spelled Djatlava or Djatlovo. No matter, really, to the 3,500 Jews and 1,200 non-Jewish Belarusians who called it home. It was a pleasant enough place but backward in the modern 20th century compared with the big cities of Poland and certainly with the modern, post–Industrial Revolution countries of Germany, France, and England. In 1924, and even until 1935 or so, Gzetl was nearly the same town with the same means of livelihood and the same lifestyle for its inhabitants as it had been for hundreds of years. I mention 1924 because, as best as I can ascertain, my father was born that year. There were records of sorts, but they were kept by the Poles or Russians or whoever happened to be in City Hall that year, and they didn't really care much about precision. In 1941, when the Germans occupied the town, they worried about precision, but even their records were lost in the war. I mention 1935 as well because by then the modern world was having an impact on Gzetl. The town had a taxi that year for the first time. Railways reached farther to the east and west, and, though the closest railway stop was 12 kilometres from the town, there were more visitors and news of the outside world coming to Gzetl. The outside world had finally started to change the way of life inside Gzetl.

For hundreds of years, life in the town had been thus: Jewish men spent a great deal of their time studying the Torah (the five books of Moses) and the many commentaries on and interpretations of it as well as the Gemorah (legal wisdom of the rabbis and sages) and in prayer. Many of the men also worked at crafts or ran small stores, but at night and on Saturdays everything stopped for prayer and study. Jewish women worked too but were not allowed to study. They knew what was needed to bring up and sustain their families, make proper Sabbaths and holidays at home, and teach their daughters how to do the same.

Marriages were arranged by parents with the help of the *shadchan*, the village matchmaker. Many women were also the breadwinners in their families when the husbands were particularly "pious" and devoted most or all of their time to study. Today it seems like an excuse not to work. In those days, it was not a laughing matter. It was not laziness that caused men to study all day and leave earthly chores to their wives. In that society, a person's standing and honour often were determined by how learned the person was. Dirt-poor rabbis who could not feed themselves or their families often had Jews from far and wide come to the town to have those rabbis solve life's major problems for them.

The rabbi's advice would be sought on matters of love, sex, marriage, commerce, honour, religion, law, and more, including matters that the rabbi could have no personal knowledge of or experience with. But everything had an answer in the holy books, so if one knew the wisdom of the books then one could advise on anything. These rabbis, or learned men, sometimes had to live on the charity of others, even eat their meals at a different home every day. No one thought this unusual or ironic. Freedom from earthly chores gave these men the time to study and become learned, and this was the measure of the person and the town. Ask a Jewish Gzetl survivor even today about the town, and almost immediately you will hear about some of the sages who made the town famous, putting it on the map of Jewish civilization. An example is Chafetz Chaim, the name given to Rabbi Israel Meyer HaCohen, who wrote a famous book that introduced the concept of *lashon hara*, literally the "evil tongue." Its precept is that not only should one not speak ill of others, but also one should not participate in gossip by listening to it.

My father was born near the beginning of the difficult part of winter at the end of 1924. Any record kept at the time of his birth is unknown today and might have been destroyed long ago. The exact date did not matter much in those days anyway, and years later he chose December 5 as his official birth date. That date was for the non-Jewish officials who used a calendar foreign to Jews. It was based on the time that it takes for the earth to go around the sun, rather than on cycles of the moon, the basis for the Jewish calendar. But my father didn't remember his birthday on the Jewish calendar either. It just wasn't that important. In the 1920s in Gzetl, they didn't have birthday parties with balloons and pony rides at which all the children in the class were invited. At least my father's family certainly didn't. Later, not knowing the date but being sure about the year, my father would lie about the Gregorian calendar year in which he was born to avoid being conscripted into the Soviet army and going to the Russian front. He was certainly not the only one who lied about his age, for a great variety of reasons. I am constantly discovering that people in those days understated their ages to avoid conscription, to attract a mate (in the case of women above the "acceptable"—frighteningly young—age of marriage), to avoid work, or for reasons known only to them. People overstated their youthful ages to the Nazis to prove that they were capable of heavy work, or other useful work, and therefore should be left to live, or to other governments to avoid heavy work or conscription because of their frailty due to old age. Today it is much harder to get away with these lies, with every bank on every corner knowing not only whether you've ever missed a payment on anything but also your social insurance number, where you work, your eye colour, your age, and of course your income. My father's sister, born about four to five years before my father, was officially, on her Canadian citizenship papers, about the same age as my father. She lied to her future husband about her age when she met him in Europe after the war (she knew younger was more attractive), and she couldn't change her story to Canadian officials when she immigrated with her husband to Canada in the early 1950s. This meant that my aunt was ineligible to receive her old age pension until she was over 69 years of age, instead of 65, even though she really needed the money. She wouldn't hear of going to the authorities and explaining why she lied when she arrived in Canada 40 years before. Not only was it shameful to her, but she also carried with her from Europe for the rest of her life a distrust of government or officials that could not be overcome, not even by her confident lawyer nephews and nieces with all their assurances. The fact is that it was much easier in Eastern Europe in those pre- and postwar days to falsify one's age than it would be in modern Canada to prove the truth and reverse a lie.

My father was born Moshe Rubin Pinsky, the third child of Baruch Lippa and Henya Pinsky who survived infancy. In the Jewish tradition, at least the Ashkenazi tradition, children are named after a deceased relative to allow the spirit to live on. For example, I am named after Baruch (my Hebrew name), and my sister, Helen, is named after Henya. (My brother, Max, is named after our mother's father.) Moshe Rubin was named after a relative whom he no longer remembered. Quickly, the name Moshe was dropped, and he was called Rubin. At the time, his oldest sister, Chasia, was about four or five, and his brother, Herzl (later known as Harry), was two. Their father was not a wealthy man by any means but a religious man and a merchant. Baruch bought produce of all sorts from the farmers in the surrounding area and sold it to local wholesalers or storekeepers. The family lived at the edge of town on a street called Slonimergasse, or the street that is on the way to Slonim, a neighbouring town. Living on this street, Baruch was one of the first to see the farmers bringing their produce to market and thus got a jump on competitors. He bought and sold grain, mushrooms, even pig's feet, which were strictly prohibited to Jews for their own consumption, but they could be bought and sold by Jews to make a living. So Baruch made a living, if a meagre one. To supplement his family's income, he had a huge baker's oven in the small living room of his house where he and Henya, but mostly he, would bake bread and sweets to sell in the street or door to door. But even in those days, there was some semblance of hygienic law, and the town's health authorities would regularly force him to shut down production for being contrary to health regulations. He was simply not permitted to bake goods in his home without a permit, which meant a monthly fee and a bribe. Baruch would dutifully cease operations and, if necessary, pay the small fine and not make a fuss. But as soon as the produce business slowed, he would take to baking again. He loved to bake, and his simple challah or sugar-sweetened cakes were in demand, not only by his family but also by others in the neighbourhood. The oven also had another use that I will reveal later.

Gzetl was shaped like a series of spokes coming out of a hub, the market in the centre of town. There, hawkers and sellers set up stalls, there were permanent shops, and there was plenty of lively activity as food, cloth, tools, buttons, kitchen utensils, shoes, and other necessities of life were bought, sold, and bartered on a daily basis. Daily, that is, except for the Sabbath. The streets went out in five or six directions from the market, with one road that connected two other towns considered the major thoroughfare of the area. Almost every street was named the street leading to the name of the next town in that direction (like Slonimergasse, the street that my father's house was on). All houses were built out of wood and crowded together on the sides for safety and to conserve space. Almost all the homes were set right up to the road, though most had a back garden of sorts. The garden was always a vegetable garden since it was a requisite of sustenance for most residents. Most people grew potatoes and stored them underground or in cold shacks during the winter months. In the winter of 1941–42, potatoes that had been stored saved my father's life. But even in normal times, when there was no war to make food scarce, without their own gardens many of the families of Gzetl would have been very hungry most winters.

The house in which my father was born was about 600 square feet or 56 square metres. After Rubin, the Pinsky family grew by one more, a sister named Rachel, when Rubin was about six. The Pinskys used all corners of the house for their daily routines, including Baruch's baking. There was a corner for his business papers, the kitchen stove (which doubled as the heating unit) occupied the central area, and the kitchen table area was also used for the parents to sleep. Two or three of the children (three when they were small) slept on top of the baker's oven. This was especially popular in the cold winter nights after Baruch had baked challah or cakes that day: not only was the oven still warm from the baking, but also the sweet smell of fresh bread still lingered in the air. The parents' "bedroom" was separated from the children by a curtain, hastily drawn after everyone had finished studies and chores for the day. There was little or no privacy, but that was not something the Pinskys or anyone else in their economic position in Gzetl expected.

Next door lived Rubin's maternal grandmother together with her daughter, Rubin's aunt, her husband, and Rubin's first cousins, Pola, Moshe, and Gedalya Krolewicki. They lived in a similar house and, because of the proximity, were very close to Rubin's family. The cousins were raised almost like sisters and brothers, the two families being together so often that they seemed like one.

When Rubin was three years old, he started to go to cheder, a preschool Bible-learning class. Cheder was conducted at the home of a rabbi who had no early childhood pedagogical education. The children were there to learn, and learn they did. If they did not, then corporal punishment was common. In addition, even the young students were subject to further punishment at home if the rabbi had a negative report for the parents. By the time Rubin was six, he could read and was well versed in many stories in the Torah. This was not particularly unusual, but in his case he had additional studies at home that many children did not have to endure. Baruch was a religious man, and on the Sabbath, or after work on a weekday (Sabbath was on Saturday, and Sunday was another workday for the Jews of the town), he would teach his children religious studies, prayers, and some of the thousands of rabbinical commentaries on the holy books. Rubin would hear the cheerful sounds of his friends and classmates playing outside on the streets and be more than a little envious, being pulled by their laughter, but he knew that studying was the right thing to do, even for a child as young as he was. At a very early age, he decided, with no small amount of encouragement from his father, that he would become a rabbi.

Not that my father never had any fun. He would sometimes steal a few minutes from study, or from helping his father with the baking or the gardening or the other chores, to play with the abandoned iron rim casing of a wagon wheel and a stick. With the stick, he would push the wagon wheel rim up and down the street, perhaps chasing dogs or other boys. This was the only "toy" that my father remembered having, but with that simple toy he was happy. He remembered his early childhood as being not an unhappy time in general. The town was safe and small enough for him to know its streets and many of its residents. His family had enough to eat and a warm house. My father was a good student and avoided the rabbi's bad books by spending extra time in study at home. His brother and sisters were at home with him, though that would soon change. He remembered nothing of that time to complain about.

When my father was six, he was enrolled in one of the four schools in Gzetl, this one being called Talmud Torah, a religious Jewish school that also taught Polish secular courses. In Gzetl, the Jews spoke Yiddish at home, prayed in Hebrew, learned Polish at school, and spoke Belarusian (virtually the same as Russian) to their non-Jewish neighbours, though many of the townspeople who were not Jewish also knew some Yiddish. Officials such as police, judges, and city administrators did not speak any Yiddish. In Talmud Torah, most classes were taught in Yiddish, but there were also Polish-language classes. The Torah and other religious studies were taught in Hebrew but translated to Yiddish for discussion. Somehow the children coped with this Tower of Babel society.

The school curriculum was double what the other children in town learned, and this tradition has stayed in our family. My parents sent me to Talmud Torah in Winnipeg, where we had a double curriculum of secular English studies for half a day and religious Hebrew and Hebrew-language studies for the other half, and all three of their children sent their children to Talmud Torah in Vancouver, with a Judaic curriculum, just as we had studied and our father before us. This is a great part of what being Jewish is about: continuity. "Jewish continuity" became the buzz phrase of the late 1990s among Jewish circles looking to keep the population from assimilating entirely.

Talmud Torah is clearly a popular name for a Jewish school, with many of the same principles of what to teach applying as much in 1996 as in 1936. But the school in Gzetl was much more religious and demanding than the schools in Winnipeg and Vancouver. Modern teaching methods preclude the discouragement of students, coaxing and teaching with the carrot rather than the stick. In 1936, teaching was forced on the children with the latter.

Soon after my father started going to school, his brother, Herzl, was sent to Baruch's brother in Kosov Poleski, Baruch's birthplace, about 110 kilometres from Gzetl. Herzl was sent to study, and study Herzl did! Living with a strict uncle and in a family that had little money to spare, Herzl rarely came home to visit and was not visited by his family, except perhaps once a year by Baruch. Today 110 kilometres can be negotiated in little over an hour or so on the freeway, but in the early 1930s in Poland that distance was a major journey if the destination was not on a railway line, which this wasn't. In fact, the closest train station to Gzetl was 12 kilometres away. Most travel was done by hitching a ride with travelling merchants on their horses and carts. The "cart drivers" for these merchants were called *furmen* (pronounced fuur-men), and they supplemented their incomes derived from hauling merchandise by taking a small amount from each passenger. The passenger would ride with the driver up front if there was room or otherwise ride with the hay or merchandise on the cart. My father remembered being taken this way to Kosov Poleski once when he was nine or 10 years old. It was the first time that he had seen his brother in three or four years, and they were basically strangers to each other. It was also the first and only time that my father met his uncle and his cousins on Baruch's side of the family. They were all wiped out in the war to come.

Some boys who took their studies seriously and finished elementary school at age 13 or so were sent to another town to go to yeshiva, a religious studies school that could offer the proper training to become a rabbi. Not all boys who went to yeshiva became rabbis, but all rabbis had to go to yeshiva to learn with ordained rabbis to become ordained. My father told me that the boys went to other towns to study at yeshiva, rather than stay in their own towns if yeshivot (plural) existed there, to make sure that they spent all their time studying, day and night.

The boy would go to a strange town or city and was given over to yeshiva rabbis who kept him in rigorous studies and gave him copious amounts of homework. The boy would have little or no time to meet others or to sneak away for other pursuits. In the case of my father, he was sent away to yeshiva because there wasn't one in Gzetl, unusual for a town with as big a Jewish population as it had. Perhaps there were enough yeshivot in the area. It was a great honour to have a yeshiva in a small town, and the Jews of each town in which a yeshiva existed went to great lengths to ensure that it would survive and thrive.

My father went to yeshiva in Molchech, a town about 26 kilometres from Gzetl. Molchech might have been bestowed the honour of a yeshiva because it was on a railway line and automatically a more important centre. Twenty-six kilometres by train was a matter of one hour. Twenty-six kilometres by foot would take all day or by *furmen* would take over half a day. Yeshiva was conducted in a synagogue with one chief rabbi and several other scholars teaching. Some of the pupils at yeshivot were also rabbis learning with greater scholars. There were 20 or so students in my father's yeshiva. Because all of the yeshiva boys were from out of town, and because there was no dormitory or other formal lodging for them, religious Jewish families of the town would accept one or more to sleep at their homes. In almost all cases, if the boy did not have to sleep in the barn with the animals, he would sleep on the floor on a straw mattress or just on straw, (hopefully) in the kitchen near the stove. This was his "home," sometimes for years. The boy would be at the synagogue from early to late, and his arrival home would be a signal that it was time for the whole family to go to bed. The boy didn't really have a corner that he could call his own, and the floor was acknowledged to be just a place to sleep. The boy's home away from home was therefore the yeshiva itself. (I keep referring only to boys. Girls rarely went to yeshiva, but there was at least one girl in Rubin's class.)

Mealtime was an even more interesting arrangement called *essen tag* or "eat days." Every day of the week my father, and thousands like him attending yeshivot in Eastern Europe, enjoyed the gracious hospitality of a different religious Jewish family in town. Sundays would be at the home of the Goldbergs, Mondays at the Levis, and so on. The boys would eat at seven different homes a week. This was arranged by the rabbis running the yeshiva with the families in the town. That's another reason why it was hard for a small town to support a yeshiva. In my father's case, the rabbis were unable to arrange an *essen tag* for Thursdays, so my father stayed at yeshiva all day and was able to study even harder that day. Luckily for him, the mother of the family that fed him on Wednesdays learned about the situation and gave him a little extra to take home with him each Wednesday after dinner. My father loved Saturday the best because he had *essen tag* at the home of someone who was relatively well off, and he ate better there than on any other day. None of the *essen tag* homes, or the homes where the boys slept for that matter, charged any fee for their hospitality. They were pleased to help make sure that the yeshiva was attracting boys who could enhance the reputations of their rabbis and perhaps one day give the yeshiva itself distinction.

A typical day for my father while at yeshiva, then, was to wake up in the kitchen of his hosts' lodging, wash, and leave for his breakfast at the *essen tag*. He would have his meal and then go to the synagogue. After an hour or so of prayer, the studies would begin. He would study laws as they were set down in the Talmud or Gemorah, laws that were not the law of the land but religious laws as laid down by the sages over hundreds or thousands of years. Hours were also spent each day in prayer to and praise of God. The boys would leave yeshiva at 8 p.m. This went on seven days a week except that on the Sabbath the boys prayed instead of studied.

Life at a yeshiva was hard, but my father loved it. He belonged to that life, body and soul, believed in it, was part of it, and knew or wanted to know nothing else. He went home to see his family twice a year, on the high holy days of Rosh Hashana and Yom Kippur and on Passover. He spent two years at yeshiva and was prepared to spend more. He went home unexpectedly in spring 1939 from yeshiva because there were whispers in the air, rumours about things turning nasty for Jews all over. Yeshivot all over Poland started to shut down. Everyone thought that there would be trouble, the extent of which they weren't sure of and couldn't possibly have foreseen. They heard about laws in Germany directed specifically against Jews. The Warsaw newspapers were full of stories about these laws and about the government in Germany that treated its own Jewish citizens like enemies of the state. But my father's family was living in Poland, and things there couldn't get as bad, or so they thought. Still, better to be with the family in times of turmoil, better to be together if anything happened. My father went back from Molchech. His sister Chasia, teaching in a town about 40 kilometres away, also went home. And they waited in Gzetl for something to happen.

CHAPTER 2

The War

Something did happen. In September 1939, Russia (already part of the Soviet Union) and Germany divided Poland into two spheres of influence. The Germans attacked Poland from the west on September 1, 1939. They didn't get as far as Gzetl, which was in the Soviet zone. Many people went through Gzetl heading for the eastern border areas and trying to keep away from the advancing Germans. Most of the people of Gzetl were in a panic: they had nowhere to go, nothing to flee to, and nothing to flee with. But they knew that the Germans were advancing, and they knew that life under them would be bad, very bad. They heard about the German laws taking away Jewish possessions and prohibiting Jews from jobs, schools, and public places; they heard rumours about German Jews being humiliated in public; and they knew about Kristallnacht in 1938, when most German Jewish businesses had been smashed.

Against this background, the arrival of the Soviet forces from the east was both unexpected and considered a miracle by the Jews of Gzetl and surrounding areas. The Jews of Russia, they knew, were relatively safe, and anti-Semitism was officially against the philosophy of the Communist Party. The Soviets moved quickly to establish their authority by putting the area under military rule under a Soviet commandant, by replacing the local judiciary with judges that it approved, and by replacing the police with Soviets or Ukrainians whom the Soviets thought that they could trust. But the overwhelming feeling among the Jews of Gzetl was one of relief that the Soviets were in control of the area and not the Germans. Most Jews, including my father's family, were determined to make the best of the situation while the war lasted. Despite the food shortages and inconveniences of war, they were prepared to bear the unpleasantness in exchange for relative safety.

The Soviet forces and their communist leaders, however, had some plans of their own other than merely to rule the area benevolently. It was in the communist master plan to make Poland a communist state, with Russia as the dominant communist partner. This plan manifested itself within a couple of months of the arrival of the Soviets through the arrest of whole families who were "capitalist exploiters." This included Jewish families in Gzetl who had worked hard to establish themselves, sometimes over several generations, and had now become so "rich" as to employ a Pole or two or several other Jews; who had worked their way into having sufficient resources so that, when a Pole needed to borrow some zlotys to pay the rent, he might go to them for a short-term loan; or who owned what would now be considered a duplex and rented part of it to others. These 12 or 15 families—the whole family, not just the breadwinner—were considered to be an influence that the communists did not want to tolerate. More than that, these "capitalists" had to be punished and rehabilitated. It was decreed that they were to be sent to work camps in Siberia and their possessions seized and distributed by Soviet order to the "people." The "rich capitalist" Jews of Gzetl were forced to leave with nothing but the clothes on their backs, perhaps a keepsake, and, if they could get by the body search, perhaps a coin stashed in some body crevice. Once they were in Siberia, the conditions were as terrible as anything that Solzhenitsyn has written about in his brilliant treatise on forced labour camps. Food was poor and monotonous, work backbreaking. The Soviet masters played horrific mind games with the prisoners to cleanse them of their capitalist leanings. Ironically, it was this forced exile and punishment in labour camps that allowed a majority of these particular Jews to survive the war. While these "unlucky" ones were being punished in forced labour camps by the Stalin regime for being anti-proletarian, their Jewish brothers and sisters were being exterminated in Nazi death camps over the next four to five years. Being deep in Siberian work camps where the Nazis never reached, those of the Jewish merchant class able to survive the harsh winters and the brute force of the Stalin regime came out of the war with at least their lives.

From October 1939 to June 1941, the Soviets controlled Gzetl with authority but not much brutality. It was nonetheless a foreign occupation, and for the remaining Jews of Gzetl the choices were very limited. Rubin and his parents and sisters often thought about leaving, but the thought itself was enough to bring back to sober reality the situation as it stood in Europe. The family had little if any funds and nothing else of value that could be turned into ready cash. The Polish currency was not readily accepted in Europe, and the Pinskys had little of it in any event. Their home was worth money only to other Jews, but those with money or liquid assets were being harassed by the Soviets. The average Jewish family in Gzetl had little, perhaps a ring or a gold bracelet, and the Pinskys were no better off than the average family. Besides, even if they had money, where could they run? The Soviets had shut off news from other parts of Poland. Yet enough news by way of travellers and letters let them know that the rest of Poland was under either Soviet or German occupation. Bordering countries were also under occupation, and there was nothing to make anyone think that Jews would be welcome or allowed in countries supposedly neutral, such as Switzerland. How could one get there even if the border was open? Travel permits were now required to go anywhere. Anyone caught travelling without a permit would be prosecuted. No, the only real choice facing the Pinsky family, like hundreds of thousands of other Polish Jewish families, was to stay and make the best of it under the Soviets. At least they still lived in their own home and could grow potatoes and other vegetables. At least they had each other, most of their friends, and familiar surroundings. They would wait out the war, and when it was over they would be together to start rebuilding. Sadly, it would not happen the way that they planned.

Baruch Lippa found that how he conducted his business would have to be altered slightly so that he would not be accused of being a capitalist "middleman." He continued to buy grain from the surrounding farmers, but now, instead of selling it at the weekly market, he sold it directly to the Soviet authorities, who distributed it to soldiers and to government-owned stores. The sales margins were thin, but in this way Baruch could feed his family when his tiny profits were supplemented with the potatoes that he grew and the baking that he continued to sell.

Under the Soviets, no anti-Semitism was officially allowed. The soldiers didn't bother the Jews much, and those Poles who had anti-Semitic feelings were on their best behaviour. As time passed under the Soviets, life began to have a certain normalcy, a rhythm that was not unbearable. The Soviets did not tolerate religion, calling it the "opiate of the people." Jews were therefore afraid to practise their religion openly. But on the high holy days, they went to synagogues en masse and did no work.

It would have been too great an affront to God not to go, and the Soviets turned a blind eye. The high holy days of Rosh Hashana and Yom Kippur were in mid-September in 1940. By then, the Soviets had been in occupation about a year. The Jews felt a little bolder by then, perhaps trying something that they would not have done several months prior. They believed that the Soviets were not monsters and that they could risk their displeasure as opposed to the wrath of God. It worked, and a few of the more religious Jews started going to synagogues on the Sabbath. The Soviets seemed to be angry but did nothing other than lecture the religious Jews on the folly of their ways. From October 1940 to June 1941, the remaining Jews of Gzetl were feeling not so badly about their fortunes in the war.

Since all the yeshivot were closed, at the age of 15 Rubin realized that he might not become a rabbi after all. He had to start thinking of a career. Early in 1940, his brother, Herzl, had been conscripted into the Soviet army, as had all the young men of conscription age. Herzl was already 18, and though short he had no good reason to stay out of the army, even though fighting for the Soviets was not high on the Pinsky family's list of life ambitions. Yet many Soviet officers and soldiers were Jews from the vast Soviet Empire and in later years from occupied Poland. Some Soviet generals were Jewish but did not acknowledge that fact. In order to rise in rank, one had to disavow any interest in religion. Most of the Jews ambitious enough to want to rise in the Soviet army ranks did not have to be convinced; they were secular anyway, especially those inside Russia itself.

"Secular" is actually not strong enough a description: many of those Jews were communists or believers that communism could save the world. Herzl was also open to ideas of this type. He saw the power of the Soviet army, he heard rumours of the situation that the Jews in German-occupied Poland faced (he didn't know the half of it), and he saw the Soviet Union as a viable alternative to the Polish regime. Having lived under the Soviets for almost a year, he and others believed that the Soviet system could work for them. To Herzl, communism started to seem better than the alternatives, and perhaps, if he were in the army, he and others could help to influence the Soviets for the better. So, when conscripted, he did not fuss, and he joined the Soviet army. He was told that his family would see him on leaves almost monthly. With Russia not openly warring with anyone, and occupied Poland now offering little resistance, army life was not the worst life that one could imagine. Being a soldier had some privileges, though not many.

Rubin was too young for the army and not of the same pragmatic or secular nature as his brother. Rubin decided that he wanted to continue his studies and try to get a clerical position when he was old enough. The skill essential for this type of career was a good grounding in written and spoken Russian. No one could get a clerical position if he could not deal with the Soviets in their own language. Rubin was good at languages. He already spoke Russian as well as Yiddish (his mother tongue), Hebrew (his language of study), Polish (the language of the street), and smatterings of other Slavic languages. But he needed practice in his written Russian, so Rubin enrolled in a night class to study the language. He was to graduate at the end of June 1941 as competent to apply for a job as a Russian-speaking Polish clerk who could also deal with Yiddish-speaking Jews. A reasonable job to help support his family looked to be a real possibility.

CHAPTER 3

Nazi Occupation

On June 22, 1941, without warning, Germany attacked Soviet-occupied Poland. The people of Gzetl heard about it instantly. The Germans were on the offensive and gaining ground fast. The town was not that far from the Russian border, and there were 10 days of fighting and movement of German ground troops, advancing toward Gzetl steadily. It terrified the population of the town. Thousands of Soviet soldiers fled through the town on their way east toward their motherland. Gzetl was not on a major road, but on a road nonetheless, and any route that took the soldiers out of the sights of German automatic weapons was the right route. Those days were torture for Rubin, his friends, and his family. Could they flee east with the retreating soldiers? What would they eat? Where would they sleep? A middle-aged man, his middle-aged wife, and their three teenaged children, two of them girls—how would they survive? Maybe the Germans would not be interested in keeping the little town, of no strategic or other value to anyone. Maybe if the Germans came in and could not find the Jews, they would lose interest and leave. Maybe the Soviet forces would hold the town after all. The Pinskys, like most of the other Jewish families in Gzetl, tried to hide while the fighting got closer and closer. They hid in the basement of their house for several days. They had no light, but they managed to store some food and did not starve. The space was small, dark, rancid, and terribly cramped, originally dug to store potatoes. But the five Pinskys stayed there for three long days and nights and prayed. They did not dare to peek out to see what the situation was. To do so was to risk capture and who knew what after that.

On June 30, 1941, the Germans captured the town. All the Soviet soldiers had fled or been captured or killed. When the German troops arrived, even though the town was predominantly Jewish, there were no Jews to be seen. The Germans had experience with this phenomenon. The non-Jews had not hidden, and the Germans required that these people, sometimes with and sometimes without force, locate their Jewish neighbours. The local non-Jews knew the town as well as the Jews, knew all the hiding places, and quickly all the Jews of the town were located. They were told to go home and not leave. Orders would be forthcoming.

Being found through the betrayal of a neighbour, the Pinskys waited at home as they were told. What else was there to do? Baruch, a religious man, started to pray. So did Rubin. His sisters and mother quietly cried. What would become of them? It was known that Germans hated Jews, that things would get bad, but how bad could they truly get? As long as the family members were together, if they had enough to eat, could they not weather this storm? They were good, God-fearing people. God would not let anything terrible happen to them. I've often wondered whether they were truly comforted by these thoughts. In a situation beyond our control, we have to say things to ourselves and those around us that will make us feel better, calm us down. Do we really believe them, or do we know in our hearts that the worst will happen? We know that we try to comfort others by looking at the bright side. It works, I suppose, but in this case, had Jews not comforted each other and realized the truth, perhaps many more would have taken the desperate measures needed to save themselves.

Within three days of the capture of Gzetl, the Nazis began to put up their decrees in public places. Jews could leave their homes, but there was a curfew of 6 p.m. Any Jews caught outside their homes after the curfew would be shot. They were not allowed to walk on the public sidewalks. From then on, they had to walk on the street beside the horses. The gold, furs, jewellery, and other valuables of the Jews were badly needed for the war effort. So were any weapons that the Jews owned, including knives. They had to deliver any valuables and weapons to the German authorities, who would issue full receipts. Any Jews found with any weapons or valuables needed for the war effort by the end of three days would be shot.

They scrambled to obey. Long lines of Jews holding all their valuable possessions in their arms were the norm for several days outside the German headquarters, at least until 6 p.m. The Germans allowed no exceptions to the curfew. A Jew who stood in line for hours to give away his valuables to the Germans had to return home if 6 p.m. was approaching and line up the next day. Violators would be, and were, shot. Nazi rules were fixed and not to be bent. The Nazis made sure that they would be taken seriously when they shot the first Jew the first day for some minor offence. The others knew to obey from then on. Jews had few if any weapons, no guns to speak of since they had never learned to use them. They were not a people who hunted because it was a sin to kill wastefully, and they could not eat the meat of animals not slaughtered ritually. Kitchen knives and other sharp instruments were turned in.

Once the valuables and weapons of the Jews were all collected, other decrees started being posted with daily regularity. To aid in the war effort, Jews had to deliver any bicycles that they owned to the German headquarters. They also had to collect any food stores that they had and deliver them. Likewise, Jews had to deposit any warm clothes at the German headquarters. All violators would be shot. And on and on and on. Every day a new decree. By July 15, 1941, Jews had very few possessions left. Nearly everything had been turned over to the German authorities, who had issued receipts for everything received. The Nazis kept immaculate records of everything.

When the decree was issued to deliver up all food, Rubin and his family faced a major challenge. It was Chasia, his older sister, who said that the potatoes that the family kept hidden, in fact buried, in the back garden should not be given up. His parents argued that it was too great a risk, that they would be shot if the Nazis found out. Besides, the Nazis would not let the people starve; they might be hungry at times, but the Jews had only to obey all the decrees in order to live. They argued quietly in Yiddish, for Jews were not the only ones in Gzetl who understood the language of the majority of the population. The family, tormented, discussed and haggled over the issue all night. In the end, Rubin and Rachel sided with their sister against their parents; this was unheard of to that point in the family, for Baruch had always had the last word. But the children prevailed on their parents, and the potatoes were not revealed to the Nazis. The potatoes could last for months under the cool earth. At the same time, both the children and the parents in the Pinsky family realized that things would never be the same in their household again; life could not return to what it had been before. In a Jewish household in those days, the father was the master. What he said was the law. The war was changing that centuries-old rule and would change almost everything else that the people knew or believed.

On July 15, 1941, all Jews in the town were required to go to the marketplace, the largest square in the town. The Germans had questioned the non-Jews of the town and had the names of 10 Jewish leaders whose names were called out. Those named included the rabbis, a lawyer, and other well-respected men of the town. The Nazis had plans for them. These men were to form the *Judenrat* or "Jewish police commission." The *Judenrat* were to implement the decisions that they themselves would make applying to the Jews of the town in compliance with the laws set down by the Nazi authorities. The Nazis said that they would not interfere with the decisions of the *Judenrat* as long as they carried out the requirements of the law and the orders of the military command. Labour would be needed to assist in the war effort. Since food would be scarce until the war ended, rationing would have to be carried out regularly. The *Judenrat* would make decisions about rationing and about the work that would have to be carried out for the good of the war effort and the common good of the Jews in the town. The *Judenrat* could choose their own leader, who would be the contact between the Jews and the military authorities.

The crowd was dismissed. The Jews of Gzetl were pleasantly surprised. Some were very encouraged. It had not been expected that the Jews would be in charge of their own affairs. Since the Soviets had taken over the town almost two years prior, very little decision-making power had been in the hands of the Jews. Some were excited about the prospects, thinking that the *Judenrat* surely would make wise enough decisions to allow the Jews of the town to survive the war and not suffer. Weren't the town's wisest men all on the *Judenrat*? These men now had power and would protect the town. It seemed that the Nazis had recognized that the best way to handle the Jews was to leave them be, to allow them to take care of themselves.

Others had doubts but had to admit that this appeared to be a positive development. Rubin and the others of the town went home feeling a bit better than they had the day before. Maybe there would be a way to survive the war in relative peace.

On July 16, the very next day, the Nazis called all Jews aged 16 to 60 to the marketplace again. They called out the names of 120 men, all of whom were not on the *Judenrat* but in other circumstances might have been. They were all leaders in their own right, either of the business community or of Jewish institutions, well-known teachers or others who had shown leadership ability or inclination. The non-Jews of the town knew the Jews well and were able to tell the Nazis exactly who fit into this category. They chose well. It was announced that these men were to pack one bag and meet that afternoon at the central market. They were needed temporarily for a work detail in Novogrudok, some eight hours away on foot. The men would be back in several months if the project went well. Food was more plentiful in Novogrudok, and the men, once settled there, would be allowed to send food and other goods back to their families in Gzetl. The men packed quickly, and the families said their hurried goodbyes. The men who could have formed the nucleus of any resistance movement, who commanded the respect of their fellow Jews and were known for their good judgment, went to the central market without protest to head out together to their new work detail. They started the day's long walk. These 120 men did not know until an hour later, and the people of Gzetl did not find out until months later, that deep in the forest of Poland the men were ordered to get off the road and gather in a small clearing in the forest; huddled in a large group, surrounded by machine guns, they were then shot. No one escaped.

Over the next days and weeks in Gzetl, the *Judenrat* started to carry out its functions. Able-bodied men and women were needed as labourers to help in the war effort. Advocate Alter Dworecki was chosen as the head of the *Judenrat*. He was an excellent organizer and had been a very successful lawyer, having won his fair share of cases on behalf of Jews, even in front of Polish judges not sympathetic to Jews, and had dealt successfully of late with the Soviet authorities. The first job was to choose those who could carry out heavy jobs and to give them a document and a red "badge" or *shein*. Those who had a *shein* were considered valuable for the war effort and had the privilege of getting additional food rations. They could also leave the town to work. Rubin was now 16 and fit. He was handed a red *shein* and told to report for his duties. He was the only one in his family who received one. His sister Chasia was not given a red *shein* since she was not strong enough to carry out heavy labour. Chasia was always short, reaching only 4'10", but would prove over the length of the war to be much stronger than anyone thought possible. For the time being, she was to stay at home with her parents and sister, Rachel. Neither was Rubin's father considered a good candidate for heavy labour. He had not worked at heavy labour in his life, and his Eastern European Jewish look of long beard, black garments, and earlocks also made him appear older and more frail than he actually was. He would not get a chance, however, to prove his strength to anyone. He was disappointed, in part, that he had not been chosen to work at Novogrudok so that he could better provide for his family. He was in as good physical condition as most of the men who had been chosen, even better than some, but he was passed over. In his mind, the misery of being separated from his family was compensated by the ability to provide for them at a time of low rations and sure hunger. Not receiving a red *shein* was a further blow to his prestige and his standing in the family. Baruch accepted this but was demoralized. The family would have to depend on his teenaged son instead of him.

Rubin was sent out to work on the road being built for the German troops and supplies to be sent to the Russian front. Every day he would leave Gzetl and go to the place where stone was being collected to lay a foundation for the road. The road had to be durable enough for trucks and tanks to cross it constantly, and the work consisted of carrying heavy stones, digging level crossings, and mixing and laying cement. The work was backbreaking and carried out in all weather conditions. Rubin worked hard and was overseen by Polish supervisors who did not often spare the rod if the labourers did not work as hard as possible. These supervisors wanted to please their German masters, for if they did not squeeze sufficient work from those under their charge they would be relieved of their command and join the labourers; besides, most often they had little sympathy for the plight of the Jews. Nazi propaganda had started to work in the area. The Nazis consistently told the Poles that the Jews had caused the problems that the Poles now faced. The Nazis played on the nationalistic feelings that Poles had against the Soviets, and in part the Poles were getting revenge on the Jews for the Soviet invasion of Poland. The Nazi propaganda machine repeatedly told big lies that the Jews were in charge of Soviet Russia and had masterminded the Soviet invasion of Poland. The Nazis told the Poles, implausibly, that they had to invade Poland to save Poland from the Soviet communists. These lies—combined with the general antipathy of many Poles toward Jews and the fear that the Poles had of Nazi guns—made the job of overseeing the Jewish workers particularly suitable for the Poles.

The *Judenrat* were given a set food allocation for all Jews in Gzetl. The *Judenrat* deliberated long and hard and came up with a fair rationing allocation, but it was barely enough to keep the labourers fed to a level that they could work effectively and all others with enough to survive. But the rationing was promised to be temporary, and the food would suffice to keep everyone alive, provided that there were no drastic changes. The *Judenrat* were also to account for the Jews on a daily basis to ensure that all labourers returned each night and that no others escaped. Any attempt to escape or leave the town without permission resulted in severe punishment not only for the perpetrator but also for the family of the perpetrator. Of course, the *Judenrat* tried to hide the fact that any escape had been attempted or any other problem had arisen that might cause the Jews trouble: disobeying, attempting to escape, lying, hiding food or weapons, or any other infraction would result in collective punishment not only for the families but also for all Jews in the town. The *Judenrat* were convinced for the time being that cooperating with the Germans was the best way for the town to survive the war. This was made abundantly clear when punishment was meted out by the Nazis for the most trifling of contraventions. Any Jews caught out after curfew, or who possessed any contraband goods, were summarily shot. Any smuggling of food would result in the denial of rations for an extended period and jail time. Smuggling of weapons would result in torture and horrible death, and the family of the smuggler would often face the same punishment. In the fall and winter of 1941, cooperation was the preferred route to survival.

Thus passed the first half year of occupation of Gzetl for its Jews: hard work, small rations, difficult decisions for the *Judenrat*, and cruel retribution for any transgressions against increasingly tough laws. Laws came into existence every so often that deprived the Jews of more rights, of more dignity, of most of their possessions. The Jews of Gzetl, however, were poor and did not own much or any silverware, jewellery, or art. Once any valuable possessions had been stolen, their remaining meagre possessions were not highly sought after by the men of the Third Reich; however, local peasants were happy to steal what they could and did so when given a chance. Yet Nazi justice was as cruel for the local Slavic population as it was for the Jews, and the Nazis did not hesitate to mete out punishment against Poles for theft or other petty crimes, including execution for many of the same "crimes" as the Jews. Therefore, the *Judenrat* could count on a certain amount of stability if they cooperated with the Nazi authorities. This gave them the false hope that cooperation would save the greatest number of Jews. That did not prove to be the case.

On February 22, 1942, only eight months after the Nazi occupation, Jewish and Polish workers were forced to build a fence around certain streets of the Jewish area of Gzetl. Rubin was away working on the highway for several days and came home to find that all Jews had been allocated places in homes inside the fenced "ghetto." The Pinsky family had been allocated part of a house now home to 60 people but only 800–900 square feet (74–84 square metres) in size. There was barely room to move, let alone sleep. It had been the house of a Jewish family, and the owners were to live there together with all the strangers who had to make it their new home. The size of the Jewish area of the town was being reduced, according to the Nazi authorities, so as to ensure order and to make military and civilian orders easier to disseminate. The Jewish fenced-in area was about three square blocks. The Jews had been given an hour's notice and told to take only those things that they could carry with them. These small possessions would have to suffice until further orders. There were never to be any orders to allow the Jews to leave, or gather the remainder of their things, but they did not know this at the time.

Rubin's house was not included in the ghetto. No one without a valid permit was allowed outside the ghetto. Rubin was the only one in his family who could leave the ghetto legally since he had to work outside Gzetl. His red *shein* saved the lives of the Pinsky family for a little while. When Rubin went out to work, he sometimes got a chance to sneak into the area of town where his house stood. On the door was a sign that the house had been confiscated by the Nazi authorities for military purposes. Many of the other Jewish houses had the same sign. Over the next several months, many local peasants took over the houses of many Jews. The Pinsky house was not one of them. The house was not so much bigger or better than most other available houses that anyone who could have it actually wanted it, and this turned out to be very fortunate for the family. Rubin could go from his work to his home on his way back to the ghetto. There he would wait until dark during the months of short daylight and dig up some potatoes in the yard without being seen since no one lived in the house. He carefully hid the potatoes in his clothes or inside the bundle of wood that he was allowed to take into the ghetto for fire fuel. The Pinskys lived on their small legal rations and secretly on these potatoes. If anyone knew of the potatoes, then they might be jealous and give away the secret to the wrong people. Smuggling of food into the ghetto was severely punished, and the Polish guards often took bribes before allowing the punishment to take place. If the guards found out, then they merely took their cut of the spoils, usually the lion's share. But if the booty was too small, not worth bothering about, or if more than one guard knew of the infraction and therefore could report the other, then the punishment could amount to torture or death.

Once in the ghetto, the lives of the Jews began to be unbearable. Rations were constantly cut so that food could go to the soldiers fighting at the front, or so said the Nazis. Living with 60 people in a small house was worse than any prison, and strict curfews on going out of the house were still enforced. Alter Dworecki, the head of the *Judenrat*, began to see that cooperation could lead to nothing but the destruction of his people. He was privileged to be able to leave the ghetto for work and used that privilege to secretly form the Jewish partisan group that would operate in the area. He quietly made contact with the few Jews who hid in the forest and tried to help them organize partisan groups. Dworecki had the cooperation of the others in the *Judenrat*, and even the chief of the Jewish police was involved. There was very little that could be done. There was not enough to feed the Jews of the ghetto, and there was nothing to spare for the partisans. However, whenever a weapon of any kind found its way into the hands of a Jew in the ghetto while out on work detail (even an old, worn-out, thrown-away part of a gun), it would find its way into the hands of the Jewish partisans. The wise men of the *Judenrat* could now see that the Jews would be treated very badly by the Nazis, so whatever could be done to resist them had to be done. The problem was that there was very little to be done. The people of the ghetto had almost nothing left with which to resist. Their energy was very low because of a lack of food and overwork. By then, the crowded living conditions and the poor sanitation were causing considerable illness. Their immune systems were weak. And of course any small instance of resistance against the Nazis or their Polish and Ukrainian guards was met with brutal and swift retribution, even murder. Dworecki realized that resistance had to be organized secretly. But it would take time. More Jews could have escaped to the forest, but they did not try to do so because of the risks. They knew that, if they did not starve to death in the forest, unfriendly peasants would give them away to the Nazis. The worst of the anti-Semitic peasants might shoot them or assist the Nazis to hunt them down. The Jews needed time to set up a support network in the forest before it would be safe to flee the ghetto. They didn't know it, but time was a luxury that they did not have.

Some others in the ghetto had also managed either to smuggle food in on a regular basis or to bribe others to do it for them, or they bought food from their guards at incredibly steep prices using hidden assets or promises of goods from relatives in America. Still, the Jews of Gzetl were not getting enough to eat. They were losing their strength, both to work and to resist. They were tired, mortally tired, and it took all their strength to survive. Degradations were inflicted in increments so that each seemed to be not so much worse than the last one, but if looked at overall they seemed to be too horrible to contemplate. These degradations included physical beatings, spitting on Jews as they passed, insults, kicks, cutting the hair of men and women, including locks worn as a religious custom, and on and on.

The question asked most often is why was there no major resistance to the Nazis among the Jews? The answer is that there was. The head of the *Judenrat*, Alter Dworecki, and the head of the Jewish police, Avraham Alpert, helped to organize secretly a resistance to the Nazis while pretending to cooperate with them. These brave men came up with elaborate plans to attack the Nazis with old, broken weapons as soon as some could be acquired. Dworecki and Alpert and others worked feverishly to acquire weapons with which to attack the Nazis. Any attack without weapons would immediately fail and result only in the deaths of the perpetrators and collective punishment for other

Jews. The main plan, then, was to purchase arms from friendly parties, or others willing to do business, and then stage a surprise attack against the Nazis. In the confusion, the Jews of the ghetto would flee to the forest and form a partisan unit. Contacts were made with Polish and Ukrainian partisan groups to try to acquire the arms.

On April 29, 1942, Shalom Piulun, a Jew from the ghetto with a red *shein* to work outside the ghetto, met with a Polish partisan group to consummate a deal to purchase some handguns and old rifles. The Jews of Gzetl had handed over almost all their remaining valuables; however, despite the orders to turn such valuables over, some still hid from the Nazis in ingenious places jewellery, silverware, gold coins, and so on. Now the Jews were prepared to give everything up so that the resistance could purchase the weapons. The price for the old weapons seemed to be high, as expected, but they were all that were available. The weapons purchased would have to be enough to carry out the plan. It was not necessary to kill many Nazis and their collaborators, only to create a diversion in which the Jews could leave the ghetto and get to the woods. Piulun met the Poles at the appointed place and time; checked the weapons, which were as agreed; handed over the money; and started to leave when he was surrounded by Nazi storm troopers. He had been set up. Piulun was taken immediately to Nazi headquarters and tortured; the Nazis wanted him to give up the names of the other Jews in the resistance movement. When he did not arrive with the weapons at the appointed time, Dworecki and the others knew that something had gone dreadfully wrong, and the chances were that Piulun had been betrayed and captured or killed. The resistance leaders also knew that their lives were in grave danger, because Piulun would likely break under torture and disclose their names. They made plans to flee to the forest. They decided to leave under the cover of darkness that night. All that day they hid in a place that would give them the easiest access to escape if the Nazis entered the ghetto.

That night a note was smuggled out of the Nazi headquarters. It was written in blood. It reached the resistance leaders as they were getting ready to leave their town after sunset. If Piulun had betrayed them, then all the Jews in the ghetto were in danger, because the Nazis would surely inflict collective punishment. If Piulun had not said anything, then perhaps the Nazis would not know that he was from Gzetl. The note said "I did not betray you; go to the forest and avenge my blood." The leaders of the resistance, seven of them, now had to decide whether to follow this advice or to stay with the 2,500 or so other Jews in Gzetl and try to protect them with what influence they had on their Nazi masters. Thinking of their situation in these terms, they realized that they were only carrying out Nazi orders and could not really help. They fled immediately to the forest to try to join the partisans.

The Jews of the town were fatigued and hungry, and their resistance was low, but until then they still had a little hope that they just might survive the war in the same way that they had survived until then. But things quickly changed. On April 30, 1942, at 5 a.m., hundreds of Nazi soldiers with German shepherd dogs and rifles burst into the ghetto and screamed at the Jews to get out and go to the town's cemetery. "Juden Raus" was the shrill order that would leave millions of corpses in its wake. Several soldiers hammered on the door of Rubin's home, and when the door opened they entered and pushed everyone out the door. They were to go to the cemetery and await further orders. Those who didn't move fast enough, even the old and infirm, were treated to a sharp reminder from the butt of a rifle or a boot in the back to encourage them to get on with it. At that time in the morning, having just been jolted out of sleep, with screaming soldiers who want immediate obedience, with snarling dogs snapping at your heels, you do as you are told. No time to think, no time for a plan. Just move, get there, stop the panic, and keep the family together, at all costs, keep the family together.

In less than an hour, all the Jews of the ghetto were assembled at the town cemetery. No one knew what the orders would be, but the way that the Nazis were acting it had to be something serious, some emergency. Most of the townspeople knew nothing about Piulun and his setup or the plan to purchase weapons. Rumours were rampant, but the truth at this stage was not something that anyone considered seriously. Finally, orders were shouted, even though other than the barking dogs there was not a sound that had to be shouted over. The Jews would be divided into two groups. One group would continue to work in Gzetl as they had been doing; the other group, mostly those who did not have meaningful work in the town, would be resettled for work elsewhere. Those chosen to be resettled did not have to pack or take their belongings. They would get new clothes when they arrived at their new work camp; anyway, they would be back in several months after their work detail was completed to get their belongings. Everyone named was to go single file through the line and go to either one side or the other.

They all knew in their hearts that this was very bad news indeed, but they couldn't bring themselves to believe that half of them were about to be slaughtered in cold blood. Who could blame them? They wanted to believe that they were useful and important to the war effort and that it was not logical that they were to be killed. In fact, it has been well documented in many studies that the Nazis were well prepared to sacrifice their position in the war in favour of their relentless desire to exterminate the Jews of Europe. Many times work important to the war effort was sacrificed in order to kill more Jews, faster and faster. Troops, transports, and weapons were used for the extermination of Jews that could have been used for the defence of Nazi field positions. In almost every case, the infamous SS, the Nazi storm troopers, forced otherwise brilliant German military men to choose the killing of Jews over the defence of Germany. This fact alone was one of the compounding factors that led to such a devastating defeat of Nazi Germany in 1944 and 1945.

In the early morning of April 30, 1942, Rubin did not know that half of the Jews of Gzetl would die within a few hours. He did see, though, that those like him, with a red *shein*, and their spouses were being sent to one side, whereas the old, the very young, the feeble, and those who had no other role in heavy labour were being sent to the other side. Rubin could see that he would not be sent away but that everyone else in his family would be. He could not bear it. He turned to one of his friends, who also had a red *shein* and like Rubin was unmarried but a few years older. Rubin told his friend to say that Chasia, his older sister, was the friend's wife. He took her hand and put it into his friend's, telling Chasia under his breath to play along. The two held hands not only in pretence but also as a comfort from the fear. When the friend was sent to the right, he had Chasia's hand in his and played his part perfectly. Chasia was also convincing, and the two went to the side of those who had been of use to the Nazis. Rubin was also sent to the right. His parents and his sister Rachel, 10 years old at the time, were sent to the left. At the end of the selection, the people on the right were forced to go back to the ghetto. No time to say goodbye. The Nazis announced that this necessary work detail was temporary and that the people on the left would return in several months. Everyone would be reunited. The Jews of Gzetl wanted to believe it, so to some extent they did. What else could they believe? The Nazis were cruel, but were they cold-blooded murderers? Were they not people with feelings of remorse and mothers and fathers, just like the Jews? The group on the right went back to their ghetto to get ready for the day's work ahead.

Rubin learned later, when word from the partisans reached the ghetto after several days, that the group on the left were marched only a handful of kilometres from town, out of earshot. There they were given shovels and instructed to dig deep holes. These were the weak, the old, and the infants of Gzetl. It was backbreaking work. They worked at it for hours and were exhausted at its conclusion. Their condition, of course, was poor to begin with because of the little food that they had been getting over the past months. At the end of the day, the group were made to strip off their clothes and stand beside the holes. They were shot 50 at a time. They generally fell into the holes, unmarked graves, and were covered with dirt. No one survived the slaughter. Afterward, the soldiers were given the reward of being able to sift through the clothes to ferret out any treasures that the Jews had put in pockets or perhaps had sewn into a seam of trousers or the lining of a skirt, but among those from Gzetl there was not much to be found. The shots were fired just far enough from the town so that they wouldn't be heard in the ghetto. There were several partisans in the area who heard the shots and went for a closer look. The eyewitnesses had seen such sights before, but it was almost impossible to convince those who had not seen them for themselves of the barbarity and nonchalance with which such murders were committed. Security, of course, was tight, and the partisans could not get close or even consider an attack. Their concern at the time was their own survival. Partisans would later become a more effective fighting force with the help of the Soviets, but at the moment they had nothing with which to fight. All that they could do was witness the event and stay alive so as to pass along the truth to others.

Alter Dworecki and the other leaders of the ghetto partisans did not wait idly by while this slaughter took place. As soon as they reached the forest, they made contact with certain Russian partisans and tried to organize them to attack the Nazis while they were marching the Jews to be "resettled" in the forest. I refer to these partisans as Russian rather than Soviet because the only partisans in this area were of either Russian or Polish ethnicity. The thinking was that in the confusion many Jews would be able to escape to the forest. The Russians refused. It was too risky. The partisans would be mowed down by the superior weaponry and manpower of the Nazis. Without weapons and without support from other partisans, Dworecki and the others could not do anything to create a diversion. Two days later the same partisans who had refused to help him ambushed him and his second in command and killed them. The effective leadership of the Gzetl resistance movement was no more.

Why did the Russians kill Dworecki? Clearly, he was a leader who inspired confidence. One can only guess that his objectives and those of the Russian partisans were not the same. Dworecki wanted to save Jews. The Russians wanted to destroy the Nazi military might. Although both would achieve the same end, the tactics would be different. Without Dworecki, any Jews who joined the local partisans would have to take their orders from the Russians.

Life in the ghetto changed after that slaughter. Certain Jews with a red *shein* were given the job, under Nazi and Polish supervision, to fence in half of the ghetto with barbed wire. When the job was done, the Jews were ordered to move into the remaining fenced-in area. Since there were only half as many Jews, they needed only half the size of the original ghetto, according to Nazi logic. The Jews were herded into the 20 or so houses in the newly fenced-in ghetto, and the remaining houses were abandoned. Rations were cut further. The food was needed for the soldiers at the Russian front. The workers were forced to work harder and for longer hours to finish the necessary work as fast as possible. The Nazis said that the war would be over soon because they were routing all their enemies. If the Jews would only do their work well, then things would get back to normal soon, and everyone would be reunited with their families.

Rubin and his friends were weak, tired, hungry. Hope was fading. They had heard from some partisans about the fate of their families "resettled" on April 30, but they didn't know whether they could believe it. They both did and did not. Their families would surely come back to them somehow. They worked knowing that they had to do something soon, but what and how? Over time, and with no word from the first group who had left Gzetl in September 1941, and no word even from their families, they began to believe the horrible truth. They were also convinced by then by a number of partisans who gave reports that the Nazis had killed all the Jews allegedly sent to work camps. So Rubin and Chasia came up with a plan. For two months, in place of some precious hours of sleep at night, they had carefully lifted two floorboards in the main room of the house that they shared with 60 others and had dug a hole large enough for three people to hide. Their roommates had watched, sometimes helping with the digging. The problem was to get rid of the dirt dug out from under the house.

They solved that problem simply. Rubin and others filled their pockets each day with dirt from the hole and slowly let it seep out of holes in their pockets once they were outside. Simple but effective.

On August 6, 1942, at about 5 a.m., the Nazis struck again. They stormed into what was left of the ghetto and forced everyone to the market square. "Juden Raus!" The ghetto was surrounded by soldiers with machine guns, aided by Ukrainian police with rifles. Rubin and Chasia realized that they were being taken for another selection. Even if they survived this selection, they could see, eventually they would be killed.

The hole under the floor of the house was almost ready. They could not get in and place the floorboards perfectly so that no one would suspect that a hole hiding three people was there. It would be obvious as a hiding place. Rubin and Chasia decided against it. But they determined that they wouldn't go quietly to their deaths. Running away or giving the slightest resistance was met immediately with a shot through the head. Rubin wanted to live. He was 17 years old.

He had a cousin who worked in a carpentry shop half in and half out of the ghetto: that is, it was on the border of the ghetto, and the barbed wire fence came up to it on one side and continued on the other. Its wall formed part of the ghetto fence. On the side facing the woods outside the ghetto, the building had a barred window. Rubin and Chasia remembered the building and that it had a basement not easily located if one didn't know where the entrance was. Pretending to obey orders to go to the market square, they gathered up their cousins Pola and Moshe Krolewicki and raced to the carpentry shop. When they arrived, there were several Jews already hiding in the basement. Over the next few minutes, more Jews arrived, and those in the basement crowded together to make room for the newcomers. In total, 15 terrified, tired, and hungry people hid in that basement and waited. They knew not what they waited for, but they just needed time to think of something, anything. They waited all day in the heat. They waited until night, and nothing had happened. At least not in that basement.

They had been right about what to expect in the market square. There had been another selection. Half of the remaining Jews were allowed to return to their ghetto and to work for the Nazis, and the other half were to be "shipped to another work camp." One of the workers still valuable to the Nazis was the carpenter. He returned to his shop and soon realized that it was being used as a refuge; he resigned himself to letting his fellow Jews hide or leave as they liked. He could not help them more, that would only result in getting himself killed, but he would not harm them. Maybe he would even join them once they had a plan.

By early afternoon the next day, some of the braver souls had decided that they would use the darkness of night to flee into the woods. They started filing away at the cement around the bars in the window of the main floor of the carpentry shop in order to break out and run to the woods. The alternative was to leave through the front door and try to flee through the ghetto gate, by now heavily guarded by soldiers with machine guns. Breaking out through the window would give them a head start on the soldiers and a fighting chance to reach the woods. Unfortunately, they made some noise in their filing, and a passing group of Ukrainian police heard the sounds. The police notified the SS storm troopers, who burst into the carpentry shop and caught all the Jews. Rubin's cousin, the carpenter, begged for their lives, telling the SS how all the people in the shop were useful and important to the Nazi war effort.

The SS officers could have killed them all on the spot, but doing so was not as efficient as having the people move closer to the burial ground and dig their own graves. The officers told the carpenter, "Yes, we need you, and tomorrow we will move you to your new work site. Don't worry about hiding; we won't tell anyone, and none of you will be punished." The Jews were ordered to wait there until morning. The SS pushed all of them back into the basement and put a bar on the door. A Ukrainian sentry was ordered to stand guard. Rubin and the others knew that their death warrant was signed.

Luckily for Rubin, his cousin knew the basement door well, having worked in the building for years. He soon had the basement door removed silently and crept up to the window. The sentry had fallen asleep on the job. They made sure that he was sound asleep with a blow to the head. All 15 people started to scratch as silently as possible at the cement around the bars of the window with whatever tools were available. They scratched for several hours, trying to remain as silent as possible. The job was already half done given their prior work before being caught. About two hours before dawn, the iron bars came off. One by one, all but two who were older and too weak to muster the energy to save themselves squeezed through the window and fled to the heavily wooded area only 100 metres or so from the ghetto. They were free. Free to starve or be hunted or be shot for a few kopeks of reward, but it was better than sure death by firing squad that morning. They ran and ran and ran through the darkness.

They stopped several hours later. Rubin figured that they had run 10 kilometres, most of it in the dark or in the early morning before true light. He was together with Chasia and their two cousins, Pola and Moshe, and several others from the ghetto. At full light, they found heavy bush and collapsed into a fitful sleep, all except one person, the sentry for all until the shift changed. The group stayed hiding in the bush until dark.

In Gzetl, the Nazis did just as Rubin and the others had suspected. They separated the skilled craftsmen from everyone else. The craftsmen were the ones sent away this time to a work camp, in Novogrudok, a town 36 kilometres to the northeast. The remainder were all shot, like those before them. In Novogrudok, all the craftsmen from various towns worked together for several months for the Nazis and, at the same time secretly and at night, built a tunnel from a bunkroom in the camp to a spot outside the camp some 200 metres away from the barbed wire fence. Although many of them died from the harsh conditions and the rampant diseases before the tunnel was ready, most of the craftsmen escaped to join the partisans.

At this stage, of the 3,000 or so Jews who lived in Gzetl at the beginning of the war, perhaps 300 had escaped and now lived in the forests of Poland; this number included Rubin and Chasia and their cousins Pola and Moshe. Like Rubin's parents, Pola and Moshe's parents and grandmother were killed. Pola's young brother, Gedalya, survived because he had been sent to a school deep in Russia during the Soviet occupation and spent the duration of the war where the Nazis never reached.

CHAPTER 4

The Dilemma

The night of May 1, 1942, Rubin and the others moved deeper into the forests of Poland. They had no experience living off the land and by this time were almost starving. It was too early in the season for berries to appear. They could catch some game but were not prepared to light a fire to cook the meat for fear of being discovered. They were desperate to find a group of Russian partisans to join, not only for the protection and knowledge of the forest that they would gain, but also to help extract some measure of revenge on the Nazis. They didn't know much about the partisans, but they did know that the partisans were in the woods somewhere. Rubin and his group kept moving at night until they reached the home of a Polish peasant who had done business with his father and whom he knew and trusted. The peasant fed them and then told Rubin that Russian partisans killed the Jews who tried to join them. He suggested that the Jews' only choice was between staying in the forest alone without weapons or food, trying to avoid all the Russians and the Nazis and their Polish and Ukrainian collaborators, or joining a work camp that he had heard about near Dworetz, some 33 kilometres from Gzetl, where the Nazi military was trying to build a military airport and badly needed workers. At that work camp, apparently, the workers were treated somewhat more tolerably than at most other camps. No questions would be asked if the workers arrived and were prepared to work hard.

Rubin's group was made up of young people who were still able to work if they were fed. They could see that they would not last in the forest with their limited knowledge of basic survival techniques and no weapons or other resources. They could not fight everyone. They decided to go to Dworetz and at least see what was happening there, if only to decide not to enter the work camp if the information proved to be faulty. They did so, moving only at night, lighting no fires, and starting to find roots and some other vegetation that was edible. When they arrived, they were able to speak to a Jewish worker whose job was to carry stones from one area to the new runway. He told them that conditions were bad, but there was some food for workers. Men and strong women could join the work group. This worker had also heard that Russian partisans killed Jews in the forest, and he admitted that this was why he stayed at the camp. Some workers died daily, but they were constantly being replaced by new people, like those in Rubin's group. Rubin and the others decided to join the work camp, at least as a temporary measure, so that they could get their bearings and learn more about the area and what possibilities were available.

Rubin and his group of 12 joined the work camp. As they were told, they were accepted without questions. They received no food until they had completed a day's work. The work was backbreaking, carrying heavy stones to line the airport runway for 12 to 15 hours in the heat of the day. Severe punishment awaited those who did not do their share, or worse, there was no food at the end of the day. The overseers were Ukrainians and had no mercy for their Jewish slaves. One meal a day and water. Rubin was getting weaker daily, and his feet were swollen. He did not want to stay, but he could see no other possibility.

After three weeks of this hard work, while carrying stones from the quarry to the runway, Rubin made contact with a Jew whom he knew slightly. This man told Rubin that he was in a partisan group, that the leader of the group was Jewish, and that Rubin should join him in the forest. He gave Rubin a map of the forest that showed how to avoid unfriendly farmers and collaborators and how to avoid the towns where Nazis or Ukrainian police might be. Rubin had had enough of helping the Nazis build a runway and was prepared to take his chances. He organized his sister, his two cousins, and two others, and the next day the six simply did not return to their camp after their day of work. They followed the map deep into the forest.

CHAPTER 5

The Forest

Rubin and the others followed the map. It took them several days to arrive at the Jewish partisan camp. The map had been a perfect guide. Travelling at night, they had been able to avoid all contact with Nazis or their collaborators. In fact, the partisan group was based only about 25 kilometres from Gzetl, and Rubin knew the area somewhat from his travels with his father. When they arrived, they found that the Jewish partisan group was led by Hirsch Kaplinski, who had been trained in the Polish army. The Jewish group, however, was part of a larger group of partisans organized and led by the Russians. The Russians dictated who could join the group. The groups cooperated with each other and carried out assignments together, and there was some autonomy for the Jewish group. As a condition of their cooperation, Kaplinski was forced to accept the Russian rule that any partisans who wanted to join had to possess weapons. He did accept as weapons, however, certain items that the Russians would not, such as knives and even pitchforks. Rubin was particularly lucky. He knew well a Polish farmer who lived in the area from his dealings with Baruch Lippa. Rubin visited one night with the farmer, delighted to see Rubin alive. The farmer knew that most of the Jews of the area had been killed or were in great difficulty. He was able to supply Rubin with his hunting rifle and Chasia with a carving knife. Both Rubin and the farmer knew that this collaboration would result in the death of the farmer if he were caught, but neither spoke about it. The farmer asked for no payment, even though his dealings with Baruch had always been strictly business. Had he asked for payment, all that he could have received was Rubin's promise to return one day and pay for the items; Rubin had nothing whatsoever. The rifle and knife allowed him, Chasia, and the others to join the partisan group.

For the next six months, the group did more just to stay alive than anything else. They moved at night and lay low during the day. They learned to eat whatever the forest yielded—berries, some roots, small game, even some edible shrubs and bark. They learned to make shelters from branches and leaves and to make baskets out of bark in which they could gather berries and even water. They learned how to make a fire and keep it almost totally hidden. They learned how to use the weapons that they had. They learned how to steal, raiding farmers or peasants whom they knew to be unfriendly to snatch some eggs or a chicken. They avoided doing so as much as possible because any such raid immediately gave away their whereabouts, and the slim pickings were not worth the likely consequences. They did raid unfriendly farmers, however, when they thought that they could steal any weapons, and they bought weapons from friendly sources whenever they could. Every day was a struggle, but they started to learn the secrets of living in the forest. There was also at this time good cooperation between the Russian and Jewish partisans, and the several groups of partisans under the command of their Russian leader carried out activities in a reasonably coordinated fashion.

In December 1942, things turned for the worse again. The Nazis, instead of concentrating their efforts on the Russian front where they had become bogged down, decided to dedicate several divisions of soldiers to scour the forests of Poland to hunt down Jewish and other partisans and escapees. The weapons of the Nazi soldiers were far superior to anything that the partisans had, and the Nazis searched with the aid of dogs and tanks in addition to their automatic rifles. Rubin's partisan group was one of several groups including Jews and Russians, and comprised over 150 men and women. The Russian command decided that the group had to disperse; it would be too easy to find a group that large. Until the massive search by the Nazis was over, if it ever would be, the most that should travel together should be four persons. Otherwise, the danger was too great.

The next several months were some of the worst that Rubin and Chasia, who always stayed together throughout the war, would face in the forest. Even staying within a reasonable distance from Gzetl, where they knew the woods best, they faced starvation and disease constantly. Typhus was ever present, and many partisans whom they came across were stricken with it and quickly died. There was no treatment available, let alone a cure. Other partisans were caught by the Nazis in their large-scale manhunt and summarily shot. Some farmers turned partisans in to the Nazis, whereas others helped to save the lives of Jews if they could.

One of the reasons that Rubin and Chasia were able to survive during this time when many others died is that Chasia had been a teacher for two years before the war in a town reasonably close to Gzetl. She knew some of the farming families that had sent their children to her school every day. She had been a popular teacher with many of the children. They were especially willing to help their former teacher if they could in small ways. They might find an egg for her or a little bread. In these meagre times, every bit helped, and somehow the harsh winter months from December to March passed. In these times, too, Rubin did things that he did not dream he could ever do. On a day that neither he nor Chasia had eaten for three days, he located and was stalking a rabbit that he spotted in the snow. What he did not notice was that he was not the only predator after the rabbit. As Rubin was nearing the rabbit and getting ready to pounce, he was preceded by a hungry timber wolf that had been stalking the same rabbit. Because partisans were sharing this forest with wolves, the pickings were much slimmer that winter for the wolves than they had been before. The wolf had pounced on the rabbit despite knowing that a human was nearby.

Rubin was desperate for food, and desperate men do desperate deeds. He bared his knife, and while the wolf was facedown making sure that the prey was dead Rubin attacked the wolf and slayed it with a slash to the neck. Only after his attack did Rubin stop to realize that the wolf was actually bigger and heavier than he was. Rubin was never a tall man, reaching his full height of 5'5" in the winter of 1942–43 when he turned 18 years old. At that time, he weighed about 85 pounds. He was wiry and alive, if barely.

In about April 1943, the Nazi hunt for partisans and Jews in the forest had diminished. The troops who did come looking for them were not as experienced in their jobs as those who had preceded them. As well, the partisans themselves were much more experienced at hiding and surviving than they had been before. The partisans knew by then which peasants and farmers would help them and which would betray them. Fewer partisans were caught than before. The survivors were a stronger group than they had been. Also, the Soviets started to parachute into the forest supplies and leaders, with maps and specific military targets to attack, and they coordinated the efforts of the partisans. The Russians had realized by then that the Jews could and would be very effective soldiers. The Jews could not allow themselves to be caught. If caught, they faced immediate death. They therefore fought as hard as any partisan and fought to the death. There was no point in giving up. Fight or die.

The new Soviet leaders had specific targets that the Kaplinski partisan band was directed to attack. They consisted mainly of garrisons, or posts, in the process of being established. These posts were defensive positions from which the Nazis could protect themselves and use as fortifications from which to attack their enemies. Once the garrisons were properly established, they were extremely difficult to attack. The partisan group in which Rubin and Chasia operated was given information on the establishment of each garrison in the area. They did whatever they could to prevent its establishment, mainly by using crossfire in the area of the intended garrison to prevent the workers from completing it. The partisans ambushed supply trucks and carts and stopped workers from getting to the garrison site.

To do this, the partisans had to kill people. They killed Nazis, but mostly they killed Polish or Ukrainian labourers trying to establish the posts. I asked my father how it felt to kill another person. He said that, even when he killed Nazis, there was no satisfaction in it. It was something that he had to do to survive and win the war against tyrants. He didn't even see his victims most of the time. He did not kill them in hand-to-hand combat. They were also not close-range executions of captured Nazi soldiers or collaborators after hours of interrogation. The tactics of the partisans were of necessity hit and run. My father rarely saw the face of any of his victims. He did not count, either, the number whom he shot from afar. Some went down, and some didn't. Some were perhaps wounded only slightly, others mortally. My father never stayed around to find out.

Later in 1943 and into 1944, the partisan group that Rubin was involved with carried out more complicated and essential tasks, always organized and led by the Soviets. Starting with cutting telephone wires and destroying railway tracks, they moved on to blowing up a track while a train was travelling on it, thereby destroying much of the train; to the more delicate derailing of trains; and to capturing or killing the guards and crew members in order to capture their cargo intact. By the time that they were liberated on July 8, 1944, Rubin and his partisan group had become a proficient and effective destructive force against the Nazi military. They had started two years earlier as a terrified group of half-starved teenagers.

The women in the partisan group did the same deadly work as the men. The partisans made no distinction between them in the allocation of tasks, regardless of the danger. Chasia proved to be as effective as any man in setting dynamite charges and cutting wires. The women also had duties that the men did not have. For example, in addition to partisan attacks, they served as the nurses and cooks for the group. In effect, they had double duty. They also assisted in the heavy work of hiding the group, an everyday duty. They dug foxholes big enough for a person to crouch in and covered the tops with branches and leaves. They became so proficient at it that, on returning from operations, the partisans had to know exactly where to go and even then to sound a prearranged signal for the ground to open up for the returning members. The foxholes were so well hidden that returning partisans sometimes had trouble finding them even knowing their locations.

In late 1943 or early 1944, Rubin became sick. Typhus was killing many partisans and even peasants and farmers who lacked proper medical attention. His fever went higher and higher, he became delirious, and it was clear that he had contracted the potentially fatal disease. Rubin needed rest, warmth, and medicine. Unluckily for him, his partisan group had instructions to move on, both for its own protection and to carry out a mission. Rubin was in bad shape. The leader of the partisans knew that he was a valuable fighter and decided to delay the departure of the group for a day to see if his fever would break. It did not. This was a clear sign that Rubin was not going to survive. The partisans knew that he would die anyway and could no longer delay the movement of their camp. The decision was made to move on and leave Rubin there to die. There were no spare hands to carry him, and even if they could carry him it would slow their progress to the point that the whole group would be in danger.

Chasia was told of the decision. She argued and pleaded with the leader but to no avail. They would leave without Rubin. Chasia made a decision then and there. She would stay with Rubin until he was well. The other partisans tried to talk her out of it. He was as good as dead, for he could not survive without medicine that they just did not have. Without the others, she would have little chance of survival on her own. Stay with the others to stay alive. Chasia refused. She said that she would stay with Rubin until he was cured.

The partisans left them the next morning. Chasia got their help to carry Rubin to a small ditch nearby before they left. At least hiding in the ditch, the chances of Chasia and Rubin being detected by passersby were reduced. Chasia covered Rubin to keep him warm. His fever was higher than ever. He had not been conscious for several days. She made sure that he was comfortable and well hidden under foliage. Then she left.

No one except Chasia knew exactly how she did it, but several hours later she came back to Rubin with over a litre of pure alcohol. She sat beside him, put his head in her lap, and started to force-feed him the alcohol. She had no medicine, but she knew that alcohol kills disease. She also knew that it could help to break the fever. For three days, she force-fed him, alternating alcohol with food and water. Chasia did not move, holding his head the whole time. Rubin got worse, but then, miraculously, the fever broke. He slowly recuperated, and within a week they were able to walk. Rubin and Chasia by then had amazing skills at survival and an ability to travel undetected in the forest. Within two weeks, they had rejoined their partisan troop, who were astonished at the good news of Rubin's survival. In war, not only disasters happen. Sometimes miracles happen too. Sometimes people make miracles happen. Rubin owed his life to Chasia.

The last month before liberation by the Russian army was the hardest time for Jewish partisans in that part of the Polish forests. In early June 1944, the Nazis decided once and for all to clear the partisans from the area. They brought in several divisions of the Ukrainian army to do the dirty work. The Ukrainians were well armed and well organized. They had tanks and dogs and had been convinced that the eradication of the Jews would solve their problems and help to end the war. They approached their job with enthusiasm and fervour. They caught or killed quite a few partisans, many of whom had eluded capture for years. Meanwhile, the Soviet army, which by then had broken the Nazi hold on Russia, was advancing from the east and came ever closer to the area where Rubin was operating. He knew that he and his group were going to be liberated, for the Russian partisans were in communication with headquarters and kept informed of Soviet army advances whenever possible. The problem was not only to survive but also to assist the Soviet advance by continuing their operations. With the Ukrainian army everywhere, it was as hard as ever just to survive. Sources of food dried up. Friendly farmers were threatened and afraid to help. They were watched closely. The Ukrainians destroyed all sources of food or weapons that they could find to prevent the partisans from getting them.

About the last week before his liberation, Rubin's partisan group were getting desperate for food. Rubin and two others decided that they had to chance contact with a local farmer who had previously supplied them with food and information. The partisans had not heard anything for several weeks because they were lying low. This had reduced their food supply critically as well as their line of communication. They had to know how the Soviets were faring and whether they were "safe" to resume operations. The three crept up to the house of the farmer and knocked quietly on the door. They had one rifle with a single bullet and two knives. They suddenly heard a rustling sound and saw that from behind the barn six Ukrainian soldiers had emerged, each with an automatic weapon. The soldiers had them in their sights and could shoot at will. Rubin began to say goodbye in his mind to his sister, for he thought that there was no way that he could escape.

Miraculously, instead of firing, the soldiers lowered their rifles and started talking to the stunned partisans in Russian. They said that they liked the Russians, had been forced to join the army, and had not participated in killing any Russians. They only killed Jews. They wanted to give themselves up to the Russian partisans. They said that they knew Russians were fair, and as natural allies with Ukrainians they knew that they would be treated properly. They said that they had wives and children, and they wanted Rubin and his "Russian" friends to testify that the six had saved them when they easily could have killed them. They also admitted, on being questioned, that Soviet soldiers at the front were very close, and perhaps it was only a matter of days before they would arrive. Rubin and his friends answered in Russian, said very little so as not to give themselves away by their Yiddish accents, but accepted the rifles and marched the prisoners to the partisan camp and handed them over to the Russians. They did not need revenge on these soldiers, even though they had admitted to killing Jews. The war was almost over for them. Could it be true?

On July 8, 1944, Soviet tanks rolled through the forest in which Rubin's partisan group were operating. Soviet troops followed the tanks and ran by, moving westward. Rubin and Chasia were too stunned to move even though they realized what this sight meant. They were finally liberated. For a moment, they did not know how to react. They stood there in silence, watching as the Russian front moved past them toward Germany. It was the greatest moment of their lives, but they could not celebrate. They both sank to their knees and wept.

CHAPTER 6

Postwar

After liberation, Rubin and Chasia needed time to grieve and put their lives back in order, but there was no time. The Nazis were not yet completely defeated. Both Rubin and Chasia were immediately inducted into the Soviet army. Rubin's job was to find and mobilize partisans and other recruits and take them by train to an army training base in Baranovitz. It was the largest town close to Gzetl. Rubin went near Gzetl many times but could not bring himself to enter it. The memories were too painful. Although many people from Eastern Europe eventually went back to see where their roots were, Rubin did not want to return. The pain of the loss of half his family was too great. There was nothing left for him there, not even a few potatoes buried in the garden. He had nothing left of value there. If there had been anything of value left, then it would have been taken by Polish collaborators before the Nazis were defeated. Chasia went to Gzetl to see whether there were any family photos or other mementoes at the family house. It had been ransacked, and there was nothing left but dust. Little by little, Rubin heard about the extent of the atrocities that took place in the concentration camps under the Nazis.

He worked for the Soviet army until late February 1945. By this time, the Soviets were starting to restore some order in Poland. They made all displaced persons (DPs) register with a central authority, and those born in Poland were required to go to a DP camp in the country. As concentration/extermination camps were liberated, some were immediately turned into DP camps. Many of the survivors of the concentration camps didn't even have the strength to stand up; they had lost everything but their lives. They were lucky if they were not suffering from disease, and they certainly had no place to go. Although better off than most of the camp survivors, Rubin and Chasia also had no place to go. Rubin was now 20 years old, and the only things that he knew were how to survive in the forest and how to pray. Oddly enough, though he turned away from God completely as a result of the war, he attended a synagogue regularly later in his life, even though he never really had a change of heart that God had forsaken the world. And the only time that he entered a forest again was for an hour or two walk with his children.

The end of the war in Europe was somewhat anti-climactic for Rubin and Chasia. The news was very welcome, of course, but nothing could bring back the lives of their family members killed by the Nazis. The one hope was that somewhere Herzl was still alive and would be reunited with them one day. They searched wherever they could, and they asked anyone who had been in the Soviet army whether he knew the whereabouts of Herzl or even if anyone had seen him alive. There was no word. This was not surprising considering that virtually all survivors were searching for any relatives or friends who might still be alive. Most would be disappointed, but many would continue searching well into the 1990s, never abandoning hope that somehow their loved ones were alive and could be reached eventually. This was not as far-fetched as one might think. Although there was free access to information among the zones of Germany occupied by the Western powers, many Jews were trapped in Soviet Russia for years, and not until the late 1980s could they let their relatives know that they were alive. There were cases of reunions 45 years or more after the war ended.

Rubin and Chasia registered with the authorities in spring 1945 and were sent to Bergen Belsen, an infamous concentration camp that was now a DP camp. German-occupied territory had been divided into zones among the British, Americans, French, and Russians. Bergen Belsen was in the British zone. The choices were limited. Although Rubin and Chasia would have preferred not to live in such a place, they had nothing, no money or even clothes. Since Rubin had no practical skills, he began to go to technical school in Bergen Belsen to learn a skill that might lead to a new life.

He and Chasia constantly asked anyone whom they met if they had any information about Herzl Pinsky. One day, for the first time in almost four years, they met a Jew who said that he had met another Jew who fit the description of Herzl, and he believed that Pinsky was the last name that the fellow used but couldn't be certain. He had met Herzl in the American zone of Germany, also in a DP camp. This was the best news that Rubin and Chasia had had for a long time. Chasia volunteered to leave the camp and find Herzl. She simply would find him no matter what it took. She left Bergen Belsen and went to the American side. It took her three weeks, but she found Herzl and brought him back. The three remaining Pinskys were reunited. Herzl had spent the war in the Russian army, and at the end of the war he had gone to Gzetl to see if he could find his family. Seeing that nothing was left in Gzetl, he had registered with the Soviet authorities and been sent to a DP camp in the American zone rather than the Soviet zone. This luck, compared with being sent to a camp in the Soviet zone, allowed the Pinskys to come together fairly soon, unlike others, reunited only many years later.

Herzl had not had an easy life in the Soviet army, but he had survived by his wits. His worst assignment was to be part of a garrison of troops whose job was to ensure by force that the front line troops did not desert or retreat. They were stationed directly behind the front line to catch any troops who tried to "advance" in the opposite direction. Some of his garrison came under fire when the Nazis could muster an offensive. Most of the time, after the turning point in the war when the Nazis started retreating, the Soviets were advancing, so Herzl's garrison did not suddenly find itself caught behind enemy lines.

Herzl told his siblings of one time when he caught a Soviet deserter running away from the fighting. Herzl cocked his rifle and aimed. His orders were to shoot to kill so as to discourage other potential deserters. The soldier started begging for his life, crying that he had six children at home to feed. Herzl, having no stomach to kill his comrades, let the soldier go.

Life in Bergen Belsen was tolerable by the standards of what Rubin had just gone through. The displaced people were fed three meals a day and given the opportunity to look for their lost loved ones. Those like Rubin and Herzl who did not have a trade were given schooling in trades that would be needed in a rebuilding Europe or even in a growing America. At this time, the United States was not accepting many European refugees, Jewish or non-Jewish. Not many countries were accepting refugees. Those who had Polish or Russian citizenship could go, of course, to their home countries. Most did not want to return. Even if their families had survived the war and there was something to return to, the thought of going to live in a communist country was not appealing to a large number of them. The same held true now for Romania, Hungary, Czechoslovakia, and other Eastern European countries. The place that most of these displaced persons wanted to go to was America, but it was closed to all but a few.

By this time, groups of Jews were organizing to go to Palestine to try to establish a Jewish homeland there. Many survivors of the Holocaust at first became very excited at the prospect that there might be a Jewish homeland in Palestine, for the Jewish people would no longer be homeless, as they had been for the past 2,000 years. Rubin and Herzl were approached in an attempt to recruit them. Go to Palestine, they were told, and be there to help vanquish the British and create the land of Israel. Go and work the land. There is so much to do. When the hard questions were asked—how do we get there? where would we live? do we have to fight? with what weapons would we fight? are we sure to have a country? what about the hostile Arab populations all around?—the answers were not reassuring.

Getting to Palestine was very difficult. Immigrants had to be smuggled in illegally against British rules. An old cargo boat would hide the immigrants among the cartons and take them as far as the Palestine coast. There it would let the immigrants off the boat at night as long as no British patrol boats were in the area. Rowboats would get the immigrants from the cargo boat to the shore. Yes, some of the cargo boats weren't seaworthy enough to make the voyage and sank. Yes, some of the cargo boats were caught by the British navy and sent back. Yes, some people had drowned in stormy nights trying to reach the shore. The immigrants also had to avoid the British shore patrol once they reached Palestine. If they were caught, then the British would imprison them and later deport them.

Once the immigrants reached the shore, if they weren't detected by British patrols, members of the Jewish underground would meet them—at least that was the plan. Sometimes the underground did not arrive, caught by the British, caught by hostile Arabs living in the area, or just unable to find a way to get there. Most times, though, they managed to arrive.

In Palestine, if the immigrant arrived safely, survival was the top priority, and fighting for a Jewish state was secondary. The young men had to look for jobs to keep themselves from being hungry. They had to avoid the British because, without proper immigration papers, they would be imprisoned and deported. As a supporter of the Betar, a militaristic Zionist movement that called for armed struggle to liberate a Jewish state from the British, Rubin knew that he would have to fight again. This time he would have to fight not in the forests of Poland but in the towns, villages, and deserts of Palestine, an area about which he knew nothing. He was tired of fighting, tired of just surviving, tired of hunger, tired of Europe. He wanted to go where he would not have to fight, not be hungry, not worry about being persecuted. He wanted to go where the streets were paved with gold. He wanted to go to America.

Rubin therefore made up his mind. He needed a skill or trade in demand in America. He and Herzl made a pact. They would study together, each in a different trade, and go together to the new world. They would help each other and never be separated again. Chasia was part of the pact as well at first, but by then she was an overly eligible woman of about 25, and she hoped to find a husband soon, or she might be considered too old to marry. In life before the war, a woman wanted to marry by 21 or risk being branded as an unmarriageable old maid. However, even a woman of 25 was not of such concern in the aftermath of the war. All conceptions of age and propriety and custom were thrown off kilter by the five years of ravage that all had just gone through, so Chasia at that age was not a hopeless case. She did not want to take chances, though. She "fudged" her age, reducing it by four to five years. Her personal documents for the remainder of her life showed her age to be less than her true age. That was common in those days, especially when all papers were lost or destroyed. Not many from small towns in eastern Poland knew their exact ages anyway, so if they were going to err it might as well be on the side of youth. After all that Chasia had gone through, after showing the courage of a hero, she was still concerned about men's perception of the "ideal" age of marriage.

It worked. Chasia did find a husband in Bergen Belsen. A simple man named Joe Frajdenrajch. His last name was a mouthful, but she found someone who loved her, and that was what counted. Chasia married Joe in the DP camp, and they tried to make a home for themselves in Poland. Over 40 years after their separation and divorce, for the rest of her life, Chasia still used Joe's family name, even though no one could pronounce it and even though they had been married for only a few years. She had always been strong willed. She had lived through the war without compromising herself. She often told me that she could have had it easy, like some women, if she were prepared to do "certain things." I have no doubt about that. She saved herself for her husband after all her heroic efforts in the war. Her strong will and principles were what Chasia had that no one could take away from her, and she stuck to them all her life. Unfortunately, it cost her. When Joe left her after a short marriage, she did not accept it and therefore did not make any effort to meet someone else. She ended up with no husband and no children, no one who would care for her like only a child of her flesh could. I and my siblings tried but failed. We just weren't the same as her own children would have been.

CHAPTER 7

The Nearsighted Ruse

Rubin chose to study dental mechanics in Bergen Belsen. He went to classes from early in the morning to mid-day, and in the afternoon everyone in the camp had to carry out chores. Dental mechanics wasn't something that Rubin thought he would love, but it was a trade that he thought would be needed in the new world. While Rubin was studying dental mechanics, Herzl, whom I will call Harry for the remainder of the book since that was the name he used in Canada, continued with his profession as a tailor. He had started apprenticing as a tailor prior to the war; he had not intended to be a rabbi like Rubin. Harry was not the academic type, though he was extremely clever. He was, in fact, one of the most clever men whom I have ever met. He spoke well, had tremendous charisma, and despite his stature of only about 5'2" stood out in a crowd once everyone had a chance to talk to him. I'm convinced that he would have made a brilliant lawyer or politician, but that was not to be. As it was, he was a very capable businessman, though not always a lucky one, as I describe later.

Harry had some wonderful stories about the war, not only how he had survived it, but also how he had become a leader and supplier. He would stand up to bullies and thrash them if he could, mostly with his tongue, but sometimes he would even engage in fisticuffs. In later life, he was a businessman whose world was much smaller than his abilities. But before that, he was a tailor and a damn fine one too.

About November 1947, before Rubin had completed the course to become a dental mechanic, notice came to the DP camp that qualified tailors were needed in Canada to work in the growing textile industry, centred in Montreal. Now, many years later, the immigration policy of the United States and Canada for European Jews, perhaps best called the "closed door" policy, is well known and documented in a book called *None Is Too Many* by Irving Abella. These and other countries could have saved millions of Jews if they had allowed immigration prior to and during the war. The fact that no country wanted the Jews helped to give Hitler the courage to do what he did, reasoning that, if no one wanted them, then no one would care if they were murdered. Some say that the Jews of the United States and Canada did not do nearly enough to save the European Jews, did not protest to the extent that they should have to bring more in, though it is unknown whether they would have been successful if they had. After the war, the Jews of Canada started to apply pressure where they could to get Jews out of Europe. Those who had family members alive brought them in on special family reunification visas. Those who had no family members in North America were sometimes brought in by Jewish businessmen who said that they needed the special skills that some European Jews possessed to build Canada's economy. Most of the Jewish businessmen who could bring in immigrants were in the *shmata* (Yiddish for "rag") business, meaning the garment manufacturing trade, making shirts, pants, suits, and whatever other clothing was needed in postwar North America.

The fact that Jewish businessmen were prepared to bring in European Jews to be employed does not mean that the immigrants had an easy time. On the contrary, the work in the garment factories was long, hard, and hot. No special breaks just because you lived through the war and all your family members died and all your possessions were taken. The factory owner didn't cause that horror in Europe for the immigrants; he brought them to North America. So they had to work hard to repay his kindness. It was not quite what some of the immigrants had hoped for, but it did bring them to the land of opportunity, and they were prepared to work their way to better positions. It took years, but the vast majority did so.

Canada needed tailors. How many European Jews knew anything about Canada? Rubin and Harry asked, searched, researched, grasping every bit of information. It was right beside America, much like America, just colder. If you got to Canada, then it would be easy to get to America. Every schoolboy knew that America was the land of plenty, for anyone who got there had become rich! Just leave Europe—that place of death, nightmares, and bad memories—and get to the golden land. Or perhaps close to the golden land, and then make the move from Canada to America next time. Besides, maybe Canada was a place one could become rich in, too, if it was like America. Rubin and Harry decided to go to Canada, to take that opportunity, for who knew when the next one would come along.

The problem was that Harry was a tailor, but Rubin was not. Canada also needed some other skilled workers, but dental mechanic was not on the list. At least not then. Maybe never. Harry tried to teach Rubin to sew, but Rubin didn't think that he could fake it well enough. They thought that only good tailors would be selected because the Canadian government actually had professional tailors come from Canada to test the applicants. The test would be in less than a week. Harry was good, very good, and he knew that he would make it. Rubin worried that he wouldn't. They would be separated again. Worse, Rubin would have to stay in Bergen Belsen, a place for which they had no stomach any longer but not sufficient funds to leave. Rubin was still in the middle of his course of studies. Rubin and Harry needed a plan, and Harry came up with a dandy.

Recommissioned in 1946 to transport European refugees to the United States and other countries, the US Army transport ship USS *General S.D. Sturgis* arrived in Braemanhaven, Germany, in December 1947 with the purpose of taking back skilled tailors to Canada. The country rented the ship under joint United States–Canada plans to take back useful refugees. Notices were circulated in DP camps such as Bergen Belsen for tailors to apply for immigration. Harry applied and went to the tailoring tests. He did as well as any tailor whom the Canadian immigration officers had seen. He sewed efficiently and quickly, and he knew the trade well. He could help some factory owner and could certainly sew even difficult materials such as leather. Harry was chosen from among many applicants. He would be given passage to Halifax and a rail ticket on to Montreal. He had to be at the ship on January 5, 1948, but first he had to pass all the medical exams. The doctor would be examining him and all the other successful applicants over the next couple of weeks. The doctor was Canadian, and the standard of health that Harry would have to pass was the Canadian standard; he had to be in perfect health, because Canada did not want sick or disabled immigrants arriving at its shores. Nor did prospective employers want to pay for non-productive workers.

Harry assured all that he was the picture of health. He in fact was. He had been in the army during the war and had eaten army food for the four years that Rubin had scrounged in the forest. And since the war, though a former death camp was not the place that any of them wanted to be, they had been fed and provided with medical attention as good as they'd ever had, and they were grateful for it. Since the end of the war, all the former partisans and prisoners and even concentration camp survivors had started to gain some weight and colour. They were regaining their health quickly. Looking at Harry, no one doubted that he was to be one of the lucky ones. He would get to Canada. It was like winning the jackpot.

The story that I am about to relate was not one that I witnessed of course. But I heard it as a boy from both my father and my uncle Harry, and I was so enthralled with it that I played it over and over again in my mind. I could see in my mind's eye the people, the scenes, the conversations. Although the story that unfolds below is true to the best of my knowledge, the conversations are ones that I imagined and are not verbatim. They must have been close to the real conversations, though, because the results of this story are later proven by the facts, as you will learn.

Harry was given all the appropriate identity papers to allow him to enter Canada: visa, work permit, boat ticket, and personal ID. The ID had a picture of Harry embossed on it. He started getting ready to leave. He made an appointment with the Canadian doctor for his medical exam exactly one week before his scheduled departure. Everything else was set.

The medical exam was thorough. Blood samples were taken, Harry's reflexes were checked, his throat was looked at, and his ears and eyes were peered into deeply. Harry was stripped and checked for any spots or signs of any potential disease. His heart rate and blood pressure were checked. His hearing was tested. All was perfect. Then his vision was checked. Harry saw very well but not on that day. He normally could thread the finest needle with the thinnest thread, counting on perfect vision and steady hands. On that day, though, he had trouble seeing the top line of the eye chart.

"Your vision is poor. Where are your glasses?" asked the doctor.

"I never needed glasses. That's ridiculous!" Harry acted shocked.

"I'm telling you, you need glasses. You are very nearsighted. How can you be a tailor if your vision is that poor?"

"Doctor, I never had trouble with my eyes before. Something must have got into my eye. Please, let's try again."

So they tried again. No change.

"You definitely must have glasses. I'm not going to let you pass the medical examination until you get some."

Harry looked mortified. "Doctor, glasses cost money. How am I going to be able to afford glasses? I've spent everything I have buying things for Canada like I was told—a warm coat, a suitcase, some clothes. I have nothing left."

The doctor was getting more than a little annoyed. He was not going to step out of line for the likes of a little would-be immigrant beggar. "Look, the rules say that unless you have decent sight, with or without glasses, you cannot enter Canada. I don't make the rules; I just have to report on what I find. If you don't want to buy glasses, I'm sure that there are plenty of others who want to take your place on the boat." The doctor knew that this would get results.

Harry changed tack. "Doctor, please don't talk that way. Of course, I'll get glasses. I didn't know how important it was. I'm going to buy them right now. I promise to have them by the time the boat leaves. Please, please, write in your report that I passed the medical exam. I'll have glasses on, and I'll see perfectly next time you see me."

The doctor, seeing that he had won the argument, became magnanimous. "Okay, I'll indicate here that you will have glasses. If you show up at the boat without them, I'll send you off. Your papers will now say that you always wear glasses. Now make sure you do as you're told." He spoke to Harry as one would scold a child.

Harry assured the doctor several more times and left.

In the next week, Harry and Rubin each bought a pair of glasses made of clear glass. Neither needed glasses to see, but both wore them now. Harry also gave to Rubin his visa, work permit, boat ticket, and ID. They worked hard at scraping, folding, pinching, and gluing so that Harry's picture on the ID was exchanged for Rubin's. Rubin became Harry. Harry was without identity.

On January 5, 1948, the crowd around the ship *General Sturgis* was enormous. Security was tight. The ship was to take 800 immigrants to Halifax. The ship had few facilities for them, but it was what was available to haul them across the Atlantic. Outside the ship, on the docks leading up to the boat's gangplank, the immigrants were huddled, waiting to be processed. Their family members not going on the ship, their friends, suppliers of food, ship workers, fuel suppliers, mechanics, and onlookers all jockeyed for position. Down the gangplank, long before the rabble could get near the ship, were processing tables. An immigrant had to pass inspection and be processed at one table before being allowed to go to the next. Visas were checked first by immigration officers. That got the immigrants into the next lineup. Then boat tickets. Then medical papers and personal ID papers. With the size of the crowd, it took many hours to process them all.

Rubin's papers, in the name of Harry Pinsky but with Rubin's picture, were in good order. "Harry" had the proper visa, the work permit, the ticket, everything. When he passed the medical examiner's table, his medical documents were in perfect order. There was a note on the permit stating that Harry Pinsky wore glasses. This man wore glasses. Nothing called attention to him. Rubin was processed easily early in the day. The line went on for hours after he was safely aboard.

It was after dark, and there were only a few more immigrants to process. All the Canadian immigration officers, the ticket takers, and the medical examiners were exhausted. They could soon rest. They had processed almost 800 people and had worked over 15 hours. The ship's crew was anxious to set sail. Suddenly, a man rushed toward them, to the line, screaming "They're gone, they're gone. I looked everywhere." The security guards were quick to grab the screamer, crossing their rifles in front of him and cautioning him in no gentle way to keep his distance. "My papers, my ship ticket, they are missing. Please, I'm supposed to be on this ship. You must let me on!" Harry stamped and jumped, creating a scene that no one could have missed. "I have a ticket for passage to Canada on this boat. Everything is gone. I have a job waiting for me in Montreal. My employer wants me. He will be very angry with you if you keep me out. Let me on, let me on!"

The immigration officer was inclined to have the intruder forced away at gunpoint, but that was not the Canadian way. He decided to be just. Let the man prove that he had a ticket and a work permit to enter Canada, and he could go aboard. The officer knew that it would be impossible to prove because the papers were missing. "How do we know that you had these things? You could just be making it up. Why should we believe you?"

"The doctor," Harry shouted, "the doctor knows me. He told me to buy glasses. I bought them, see? I can see perfectly now. Get the doctor who took the medical examinations."

The doctor who had examined Harry the week prior did not have to be summoned. Everyone not below deck on the ship had heard the fuss that Harry had made and was watching the action. Many of the onlookers were convinced that the screaming man was mad and would force the authorities to shoot him. But Harry scanned his audience and soon spotted the doctor on the upper deck, watching. Until then, the doctor could tell only that there was a scene but didn't know the nature of it. Now the madman was pointing to the doctor and calling him, shouting. "Why is he pointing at me?" thought the doctor.

"Doctor, look, I bought the glasses. I can see. I can even see you from here. The glasses work perfectly. Please come down and tell them. . . ."

People around the doctor made room. He was important; he could solve this problem. He started walking to the gangplank, still not knowing what this was about. But Harry kept up the banter, shouting to the doctor over and over, talking as if they knew each other well. The security guards and the immigration officers had run out of patience, but when they saw the doctor coming they didn't want to take any premature action. This jumping, loud man was not a physical threat, merely a nuisance. The doctor would set things straight. He arrived at the gangplank. "What is going on?" he asked the guards.

Harry was talking non-stop to the doctor.

"He says that you can prove he has a work permit, and visa, and passage ticket."

"Doctor, don't you remember me? You told me to buy glasses. I borrowed the money from my neighbour. I promised to pay her back with my first paycheque. I've got a job waiting for me in Montreal. I can see perfectly now. I could see you on the upper deck of the ship. Please tell them, Herr doctor, that

I have a work permit and a ticket. They're gone. That's why I'm late. I looked everywhere. Please, you must—."

"Slow down, slow down." The doctor started to take charge of things. "What's your name?"

"My name is Rubin Pinsky," Harry answered.

"Yes, I remember you. You're right, I remember seeing your work permit. The tailor who couldn't see. What happened to your papers?"

"I think they were stolen; it must have been last night while I slept. I looked everywhere. Here's the suitcase I bought for this trip, and here are all my things. Only my papers were stolen. Please, I need to get to Canada to start my job; my employer is waiting. Everything is arranged. And I must pay back my neighbour who lent me the money to buy the glasses...."

"All right, all right. Officer, I can testify that this man had a work permit. He also had a ticket for passage on this boat. He was in perfect health except for his eyesight, and I made him promise to buy glasses. You already have 800 people crammed into this boat. One more won't make a difference. Let him on."

So they did!

CHAPTER 8

Canada

It took seven days to cross the ocean. Rubin was sick most of the time. The facilities for people on the troop carrier *General Sturgis* were basic. The ship arrived in Halifax harbour on January 13, 1948. Between bouts of having his stomach revolt against him, Rubin had been able to reflect on what he had just been through. Prior to the war, he had been very religious. He had wanted to be a rabbi. Now he doubted God, whether he existed at all, and if he did exist was he not evil or uncaring to allow what had happened to Rubin and his family? Rubin was angry, and he knew that what he was about to do would put to an end the tradition and the very lifeblood of generations of his family. He stopped praying. He revolted against God by refusing to be religious. This was more a blow to him, of course, than to the intended recipient. Rubin did not know how to live life as an atheist. Yet, after thinking about the horrors that he had experienced and the worse ones that he had heard about, he could no longer believe in God.

Rubin and Harry did not stop in Halifax. They knew virtually no English and could not have survived in anything but a Jewish or Eastern European community. They got through immigration after switching back their identity papers so that Rubin was Rubin and Harry was Harry. They caught the first train to Montreal together with most of the other immigrants on the *General Sturgis*. Most of the immigrants had jobs in

Montreal to go to, and many were in the same situation as Rubin and Harry in terms of language and skills. When they got to Montreal, the Jewish community was very welcoming. The immigrants were offered cheap accommodations and meals paid for by the Jewish Immigrant Aid Society, and those who had no jobs were given leads. Harry already had a job lined up and started right away in a sewing factory. Wages were not good, but they were livable. Rubin, with the help of the Jewish Immigrant Aid Society, applied to teachers' seminary. It was for those who wanted to learn to teach at a Yiddish school. At such a school, the regular public school subjects were taught in English for half the day and in Yiddish for the other half of the day when the students were taught the Bible, Jewish history, other specific Jewish studies, and the Yiddish language itself. Since Rubin had a thorough grounding in Jewish studies, having been a rabbinical student at yeshiva, he applied to be accepted at an advanced stage of the three-year program. He was tested and accepted in February 1948 in the middle of the second year of the program.

During the year and a half that Rubin spent in Montreal, his life was very limited. His English did not improve dramatically because he had little chance to speak it. Virtually everyone with whom he had contact spoke Yiddish. He worked hard most days at his studies. He lived in a small room shared with several other immigrants and his brother. There wasn't much of a social life, but there was some. It was in Montreal that Rubin tried dating. He went out with some Yiddish-speaking girls whom he met in the seminary or otherwise through the Jewish community. He learned some English through them. He also learned some English at the seminary because it was likely that he would teach students not totally fluent in Yiddish.

Until he arrived in Montreal, Rubin had lived because of a survival instinct powerful in us all. After some time in Montreal, living became something that he wanted because the future held hope. He enjoyed human kindness, both financially (the Jewish community paid for the seminary training) and personally. People were kind to him. Rubin was a survivor. True, there were lots of survivors in Montreal, but those who showed a willingness to embrace life, like Rubin and Harry, were the beneficiaries of an organized campaign of friendliness and assistance from the local Jewish community.

In June 1949, Rubin graduated from the teaching seminary. He did well at school. The seminary helped him to apply for jobs at various Yiddish schools in Canada. The choices were limited. There were several Yiddish schools in Montreal, some in Toronto, and one in Winnipeg. Rubin landed a job in Winnipeg. It was not hard, surprisingly, for him to leave Montreal, even though he knew not a soul in Winnipeg. He had a real job, and the excitement of this prospect was enough to overcome any concern that he had. A job meant a normal life. Rubin wanted a job for so many reasons. He wanted to repay those who had been generous and shared with him for the past year and a half. He wanted to be paid for an honest day's labour because he earned it. And he wanted a job so that he would have something to offer a woman. Without a job, he thought, dating a woman was cheating her. He could not offer her anything until he could sustain her. He would never be rich on a teacher's salary, but he would be respected and able to sustain a wife and children. The prospect of a normal life awaited him. He rushed to Winnipeg.

CHAPTER 9

Winnipeg

From the time that my father reached Winnipeg, I have other sources of information about his life besides the ones mentioned to this point. He was 30 when I was born, so at the time of first writing this I had been around to experience over 40 years of his life. My sister, Helen, is three years older than me and has strong memories of family matters, so she was another good source. Others in the family, including my mother and her cousin Dr. Shia Moser, the first of my mother's family to meet my father, also have their versions of events. The list of sources became richer.

Rubin started teaching at Peretz Shul in the North End of Winnipeg in September 1949. At the time, most Jewish kids who got a Jewish education were still being taught at Peretz Shul, though the new Talmud Torah school was quickly becoming a competitor. Peretz Shul was where children were taught in Yiddish, the language of their parents, most of them having come from Eastern Europe relatively recently. Yiddish was the language of Jewish culture and Jewish humour, rich in diverse sayings and teachings, full of apt expressions and hilarious insults. It was the language that these immigrants and their predecessors had spoken for hundreds of years at home, the *mama loshen* or "mother tongue." It was also the language of the ghetto.

Hebrew, on the other hand, was the language taught at the Talmud Torah. It was the stark language of the Bible. It had been used only for prayer and study for hundreds or perhaps thousands of years. There was no culture, no jokes, no expressions, no insults in Hebrew. But it was the language of the newly created country of Israel. It was the language of fighting for what belonged rightfully to Jews, of standing up for Jewish rights. It was the language that Jews who spoke hundreds of different languages would all have to learn together. They all spoke it equally badly. Over the next 30 years, Yiddish would become the language only of old Ashkenazi Jews. Hebrew would be the Jewish language taught universally to the younger generation of Jews. In 1949, however, Yiddish was far from dead.

Rubin started slowly, but he was a good teacher. He was patient, and he knew his materials well. He was, and remained for the rest of his life, wonderful with children. His grandchildren treated him like a great big live teddy bear, they loved him so. It was during his teaching years that his sense of humour started to reappear. He was ready to laugh, and he had a quick quip that often would have his students in stitches. His sense of humour was helped along by his teaching in the Yiddish language, which seemed to have a timely expression or a joke specially made for every occasion. His teaching career, though, was not as long as it should have been.

CHAPTER 10

Romance

During his first year at Peretz Shul, Rubin had the good fortune to be a fellow teacher of Dr. Shia Moser, an extraordinary man. At that time, Shia had not yet earned his PhD. He was a teacher of Yiddish at Peretz, like my father, having come to Winnipeg a year prior from Europe. Shia had escaped from the Nazis by walking halfway through Russia and spending years as a teacher deep in the heart of Siberia, where the Nazis never reached. He had a cousin, my mother, Jenny Moser, who in 1950 was an "old maid" (according to her mother's way of counting) of 20, soon to turn 21. Jenny had been engaged once before, but that had turned sour, and the family was very worried that she would never marry and be doomed to live out a lonely existence unless desperate measures were taken. If you knew Shia, then you would realize immediately that causing him to be a *shadchan*, or "matchmaker," was desperate indeed! In fact, the only real problem with Jenny was that her parents worried too much about her and treated her as if she were not very bright. For example, she was not allowed to learn to ride a bicycle, much too dangerous and unladylike. She was discouraged from going into higher education. That was not for women; they should learn to entertain their husbands by playing the piano, and, if they had to get out into the business world, then they should learn typing. In fact, Jenny was bright, and her report cards at school were very good. She just was not encouraged to excel at school. Her intelligence was also hidden by how shy and withdrawn she was.

Shia asked Rubin over for dinner one Friday evening in October 1950. Being a bachelor, Shia was not about to cook. So he took Rubin over to Jenny's parents, Menachem Mendel, known as Mendel, and Fanny Moser, whom I can only imagine were overly anxious that they and Jenny should make a good impression. Rubin was fussed over, the best china was used, and Jenny was made up to look her best. True, she was not a beauty, but then neither was Rubin. She had the benefit of youth (21 *is* young) and an even more youthful complexion. Rubin was happy there. It had been a very long time, if ever, since someone had fussed over him the way that these people did. He found the family to be very upstanding, the conversation stimulating, all in a language that he spoke well, Yiddish. Although Jenny had been born in Winnipeg, Yiddish was her first language, the one spoken at home. Her parents, especially her mother, were not comfortable speaking English, even after having been in Winnipeg for over 20 years. Rubin, full and content after the Shabbos meal, asked Jenny out. It was the first seed of what blossomed into a marriage that lasted 50 years, until death did them part.

Jenny Moser had the misfortune of being somewhat ordinary in a family of particularly bright and accomplished people. And being female, as described above, was a sufficient reason in her family to quash any attempt at reaching the potential that she did possess. In fairness to her parents, she might have seemed somewhat backward compared with her brother and her cousins. Her older brother by nine years, Sam, was very bright and went on to become a successful businessman. He adored his much younger sister and helped his parents to overprotect Jenny. Her twin cousins, Mendel's brother Robert's sons Frank and Willie Moser, two years older than Jenny, and their older brother, Leo, were math or science geniuses, two of whom went on to become well-known math professors at Canadian universities and internationally ranked chess players. The third son, Frank, won many scholarships and became a research scientist at Kodak. Other cousins, though not all shining quite so brightly, did not live nearby, were further in age, or weren't as closely related as these cousins and therefore did not play as important a role in Mendel and Fanny's lives. It was to these people that Jenny was compared, and she came out on the short end.

Also, in fairness to Mendel and Fanny (or Faige in Yiddish), Jenny had been a miracle whom they thought they needed to protect. After Fanny had Sam nine years before Jenny's birth, the doctor told Fanny that having another child would kill her, and she absolutely should not get pregnant again. After over eight years and pining for another child, Fanny did become pregnant again and stubbornly insisted on going through with the birth. Jenny's healthy birth was a godsend for Fanny, and she showered Jenny with love and (too much) protection.

Rubin and Jenny's premarital romance was short lived. Both were incredible prudes, even for the morality of 1950. They dated a few times, and on the fifth or sixth date they kissed. That was it; they were going to be married. They both knew it. They both knew absolutely that if a man kissed a woman, anything more than the slightest goodnight peck, it meant marriage. They thought more or less along the same lines for the next 50 years. They were hooked. They were engaged in December 1950. They were married on March 18, 1951.

CHAPTER 11

Stability

Other than the fact that Rubin continued to have nightmares about the war every night for the first three years of his marriage, his life was settling down to be much like the lives of others who had not gone through the agony of the Holocaust. He had a steady job, a wife who quickly became pregnant (lots of jokes about becoming pregnant *too* quickly, but my parents were not like that, and anyway the math works for the nine-month gestation period), and they soon bought a house, about a block away from Jenny's parents. This was very convenient because, though Jenny had been treated like she should be barefoot and pregnant, her mother had never taught her how to cook. Not a bit. She could not even boil water. Her mother would come over for the first few months and occasionally bring some food. Yet she still didn't teach Jenny and did much of the cooking for her. Most of the week, though, Jenny tried to cook what she could on her own. Rubin was not by nature a complainer, and I can attest to the fact that he would eat just about anything, the hotter temperature-wise the better, but Jenny's cooking in the first years of marriage was too much. After a year of holding in his complaints, Rubin blurted out one day that her cooking was not tasty, that Jenny would starve him with her horrible food if he let her, and he was not going to take it anymore. Jenny was horrified. She had married a quiet, dignified teacher who had never had an outburst like this before. There were precious few such outbursts in their 50 years together. She went crying to her mother and the next day enrolled in a cooking class. Rubin ate Fanny's boiled chicken for the next few months, but it was better than the alternative. Jenny eventually got to know what Rubin liked, which included most anything that wasn't burned to a crisp, as it turned out. She became a decent cook in time and in fact reasonably creative.

The relationship between Rubin and Jenny's parents cannot be overemphasized. From the start, Mendel and Fanny treated Rubin like their own son; they adored him. He responded willingly and acted toward them as if they were his own parents. He was a wonderful son-in-law: intelligent, willing to work hard, considerate, good to their daughter, and he had a profession. They in turn were wonderful parents-in–law, helping the newlyweds in any way that they could, doling out appreciation and love, giving advice. It was a mutual admiration society that lasted throughout their lives.

Mendel had started a work shirt factory—Mid-West Garments—in Winnipeg in the 1930s with three broken-down sewing machines. He had started with virtually nothing and, like many immigrants before him, had built the factory with his efforts and his brains. Profits and cash flowed back into the business, always making it better and more stable. Mendel had taken his son, Sam, into the business, and by 1954 they had over 30 employees. Rubin saw the growth of the business in the three years that he had known Jenny. He also realized that for him being a teacher was a dead end. No room for improvement. No way to reach the top. No way to afford the kind of material goods that he thought he should have for his family. He asked Mendel to take him into the business.

There were lots of considerations in Rubin's request that complicated the decision for Mendel. First, Rubin was obviously a bright man, and Mendel could always use a bright man. But, he figured, Rubin would want to be a boss very soon, and there was room for only one boss. Sam was the next boss after Mendel; there could be no question or controversy over that. He didn't want that anyone should be a natural rival to Sam, especially someone in the family, because that could lead to family troubles. Yet Rubin was ambitious and would not settle for being a teacher for long. If Mendel did not help his son-in-law, then Rubin might always be unhappy and feel unjustly treated. Mendel also wanted more for his daughter than a teacher's salary could afford. He talked to Sam.

Sam Moser was one of the nicest, kindest men whom I ever met; he always tried to do the right thing, the generous thing. He also was unencumbered at that time by a family of his own, which sometimes can dissuade a person from otherwise magnanimous acts (Sam later married a woman as magnanimous as he was). He thought that he could handle working with Rubin in the same small factory, both under the leadership of Mendel. They were ready to accept Rubin, and he was told the good news. There was one additional wrinkle, however, that Mendel and Sam were not aware of: Jenny was happy with Rubin as a teacher. A teacher was whom she married, and she wanted to stay married to one. Teachers came home after school ended in the afternoon and mostly did not work until late and on weekends. She didn't understand (no one ever bothered to explain to her) the business that Mendel and Sam would discuss (boringly to her) at the dinner table. She knew full well how businessmen operated, leaving their wives for hours on end for their business (potentially worse timewise than a mistress). The election was over, but Jenny didn't get to vote. She heard the news, biting her lip for Rubin's sake. She was worried but at that time did not make a fuss. She trusted her husband, her father, and her brother.

Rubin taught for only three years and could have been happy as a teacher for the rest of his working career if it were not for one thing: ambition. He wanted more for himself and his family. He was prepared to work very hard and to make something of himself; he wanted to be someone who could hold his head high by providing well for his family. In the end, he did not listen to Jenny, who was perfectly content and would always look up to him as a teacher, a profession that she thought very honourable. In fact, that was a good part of the reason that she married him. But he was not satisfied, so three years were all the teaching that he would ever do. In the end, Rubin turned out to be a rolling stone.

My father was starting a new life in more ways than one. On December 22, 1951, my sister was born, my parents' first child. Helen was a baby who always knew what she wanted and how to achieve it (a quality that she successfully harnessed many times in life), and she was the apple of his eye. He was wonderful with her, and she became his special treat. In the 1950s, men were not in the habit of attending the birthing room, and my father didn't even dream that he might do so. He knew little or nothing about giving birth in Canada, but he sure could change diapers, with zeal. He was happy to do all the chores that he could to be closer to his newborn daughter. This carried on with his other children as well. My father would cheerfully dress me in the mornings for more than a year after I was perfectly capable of dressing myself. I was lazy, and that gave him the excuse to tickle my feet and play with me first thing in the morning as part of dressing me. He was a great dad, and remained so to the end, but his time with us was limited, especially starting in 1960.

I was born in September 1954 and my brother, Max, in November 1958. This rounded out the family that our father had sought. He had a daughter and two sons, and things were relatively good. Our parents were happy. They had something in common that few couples their age had. Both were like immigrants, not so much in terms of language, since our mother's English was native, but in their shared old country attitudes and morality. Our mother had been so protected in her family's cocoon that she knew little more of the ways of the "new world" than our father and sometimes less. She also learned from him, the adventurous one of the couple. He had survived for years in the forests of Poland. She was sure that he could handle anything that came up. She respected him immensely.

In 1956, Rubin and Jenny bought a house on Royal Crescent in Winnipeg, the last street on the north side in the newish neighbourhood of West Kildonan. The house was new, a rancher, with three bedrooms on the main floor and a full unfinished basement. The yard was huge, with lots of room for the kids to play and lots left over for Rubin to garden. The house was pivotal in his life because it was a symbol that he was now successful. He bought the house for $15,000, a lot of money for him in 1956. He was so proud. This was his land, his kingdom, and he had earned it (or would earn it by paying the mortgage payments) himself. Our family lived there for 14 years.

In 1954, Rubin got the job of chief shipper at Mid-West Garments, a business that continued to grow. He worked there for six years. He was happy there at first, but true to his immigrant blood over time he wanted to be his own boss. Problems also developed in late 1956. Mendel suddenly had stomach ailments. On examination, the doctors knew that it was stomach cancer and was quite advanced. He had worked hard for many years to build a successful business, and if there was any time that his success might help him it was now, he hoped. He got on a plane to head to the Mayo Clinic in Rochester, Minnesota. The clinic was world renowned, particularly in nearby Winnipeg, as having the most advanced medical facilities in the world. If anyone could help Mendel, the doctors at the Mayo could. He was there for about three weeks. At first, the treatment seemed to be working. Suddenly, though, he took a turn for the worse and died in March 1957. He never went home from the Mayo Clinic. He was 65.

The shock to the family was severe, for they had been close. Jenny was devastated. Fanny, who had spent all her days in Canada in her own house, virtually never venturing out and leaving all dealings with the outside world to Mendel, was worse. She would never get over her husband's death and relied as much on her son and daughter from then on as she had on her husband. Don't get the wrong idea, for Fanny was no wallflower. It was just that she ruled in her home but was not interested in what went on outside it. She would entertain, cook, and keep a clean and warm house, but most of what went on outside it was to her a man's world, and that included buying insurance, paying bills and taxes, and so on. She just decided that it was not her domain.

Mendel's passing complicated Rubin's life as well. Sam became the boss at Mid-West Garments. He was a wonderful employer and a fine man, but indirectly through Fanny's ownership Jenny now had a minority interest in the business. Sam had the right to buy out Jenny's shares, which he eventually did. Rubin did not feel hard done by, only that he, too, would like to be a boss. The situation continued for a few years until an opportunity presented itself.

CHAPTER 12

Business

In 1959, Jenny's first cousin Izzie Moser, very successful in business to that point, wanted to sell one of the smaller parts of his business. This was the business of making chamois, the soft leather from deer hide that in those days was the most common lining of winter coats. Chamois was also used as a soft cloth to clean cars, dishes, and anything else that might be scratched by rougher materials. Those were the days before disposable towels. The business consisted of buying scrap chamois pieces and contracting out the piecework of sewing the scraps together into large rolls of smooth chamois so that in turn they could be cut into coat lining or washcloths and sold. Rubin still knew nothing about sewing and how to supervise a group of subcontractors who did it, but he knew someone who did have that expertise. He called Harry, still sewing in a garment factory in Montreal, and offered his brother a partnership. Harry was to come to Winnipeg. Rubin would take care of buying the business. They would go into the business together and grow it.

Rubin had no money saved with which to buy the business. It was not that expensive, but whatever it was he did not have. He had four dependants and was living on a reasonably modest salary; what he didn't spend on the family went to pay the mortgage. True, Sam was going to buy out Jenny's portion of Mid-West Garments, but that payout was to be over a period of years and would occur only after Fanny passed away. While she was alive, the profits from the business had to support her, for she had no other means of livelihood. Rubin went to Izzie and offered him the full price for his business. Rubin asked Izzie to carry 100 percent of the purchase price, with full interest being paid monthly on the outstanding balance. Izzie had never done business this way before and was somewhat taken aback. There was no security. Rubin said that the security was his marriage to Jenny. He would never let a Moser down. Izzie thought about it and, knowing that Rubin was a man of his word, agreed.

Harry moved to Winnipeg from Montreal. He was still a bachelor and ready to work hard. Rubin gave his notice to Sam, and in early 1960, in a room rented from Shadick and Company, realtors and insurance brokers at 175 Donald Street in downtown Winnipeg, Rubin and Harry entered the chamois business. They went on buying trips to acquire chamois scraps; contracted out the sewing of the scraps into larger pieces (mostly done by housewives who could fit in sewing on their home machines at odd hours); picked up the stitched-together chamois from those sewers; dropped it off with and supervised other sewers who made larger rectangles for washcloths and rolls on 36-inch cardboard tubes for coat lining; packaged the washcloths for retail sale; and made trips to coat manufacturers throughout Canada to sell the rolls for lining. Rubin started to travel, which did not sit well with Jenny, who had three young children at home. But that is what the business demanded. Harry travelled more because he was still single for the first few years of their partnership. Soon Rubin and Harry added sponges to the business. They bought dried and pressed sponges and rehydrated them. These they would dry as full-sized sponges and package them for washing dishes or any other type of washing by hand that didn't need the soft touch of chamois. This was hard work and demanded long hours of the partners, and unfortunately they were not growing businesses. Rubin and Harry went into the business at a time when artificial products (J-Cloth and other fabrics, for example) were starting to appear on the market. The 1960s were not like now, when natural fibres and products are highly prized. The 1960s were a time when artificial products were the eighth wonder of the world, and anything synthetic was considered to be superior to the products that nature provided. Rubin and Harry were making a living—but just.

They believed instinctively and came to the decision at essentially the same time that a man (in those days, they thought that this applied only to men) could not be anything in the world unless he owned land. They decided that they would acquire land and hold it for as long as they could. Over time, it would appreciate in value. Although they could not make substantial sums at their business, they could make enough to live on. They planned to accumulate land somehow and over a period of years sell it so that, when the opportunity arose, they could sell their business and get into something else. The idea was a good one. The problem was that they had it in Winnipeg in the early 1960s. The city was then at its zenith as an important Canadian centre. Relative to land values in the rest of Canada, Winnipeg's prices were the highest that they would ever be. In the early 1960s, the city was still the entry hub of the west. Students from western Ontario, Manitoba, Saskatchewan, and Alberta went to Winnipeg to study at the University of Manitoba. Winnipeg was the third largest city in Canada. Its manufacturing sector was thriving in the time before cheap Asian imports closed most of its factories 20 years later. The Winnipeg International Airport was built with the knowledge that cross-continental flights, such as New York to Los Angeles, had to stop in Winnipeg to refuel. The Jewish community was over 19,000 strong, and most of its members thought that the community would continue to grow together with the rest of the population. They thought that real estate in and around Winnipeg was where money could really be made. Boy, did they have the wrong number! Parcels of property that my father bought in 1961 and 1962 had the same value in *actual dollars* in 1996. Land that cost $700 an acre in 1961 cost $700 an acre in 1996, when I first wrote this book. This was *after* paying taxes every year, making repairs, trying to find tenants, dealing with delinquent renters, and so on. Real estate in Winnipeg was Rubin and Harry's chosen path to fortune, but it didn't work out as well as it would have most anywhere else.

Anyone who says today that small businesspeople must pay more taxes, that they get all the breaks, that there are too many loopholes for business do not get a sympathetic ear from me. As I grew up, my father was most often gone from the house before I woke up for school, and he often came home from work long after I went to bed. He and Harry were trying to keep three businesses operating. After chamois and sponge products were established, they created a real estate business. But how were they to buy real estate with no capital? Solution: earn it as their sales commission.

One after the other in 1961, Rubin and Harry studied at night to earn their real estate broker's licences. It was not as complicated then as it is now, and both managed to pass within six months of having their real estate brainstorm. They bought the business Shadick and Company from Mrs. Shadick, the widow of the previous principal of the realty and insurance brokerage, on payment terms that would depend on their success. In the same little rented house from which they operated their other businesses, they hung up a new sign, "R & H Agencies Ltd" (for

Rubin and Harry) in place of Shadick and Company. Between going on buying and selling trips, packaging sponges and rolling chamois, they tried to sell real estate in Winnipeg. They also came up with a plan for how they could participate themselves. When they found a parcel of land for sale that looked to them like an attractive long-term hold, they would form syndicates of doctors or other investors to acquire it. They would handle the management of the property so that it would be a worry-free investment for those who supplied the capital. Rubin and Harry would take their commission as a percentage of the property, no cash commission. If the property made no money for the investors, then it made none for Rubin and Harry too. It was an attractive enough proposition to investors that over the next several years the two were able to syndicate several parcels of agriculturally zoned property that "just needed to wait a few years" so that the city would grow to include the agricultural land. The plan was that the land would eventually be rezoned for development and sold at a substantial profit.

The problem was that Winnipeg just stopped growing. New planes could fly non-stop from New York to Los Angeles, no refuelling in Winnipeg necessary. Universities, and more importantly jobs and businesses, developed quickly in Alberta and British Columbia, not in Winnipeg. Toronto was in a much better geographic position and becoming a major rival to Montreal as Canada's largest city, attracting much greater growth. Asian and other imported clothing started to take a bite out of Winnipeg's manufacturing sector. The agricultural sector, Manitoba's biggest employer, was about to begin a slide toward a low point matched by a corresponding real estate slide. Wheat prices in the 1980s and 1990s were lower in actual dollars than they were in the mid-1960s taking inflation into account. Winnipeg's other major disadvantages—being bitterly cold in winter, overrun with mosquitoes in summer, too small a market, and just too darn far from everything—started to catch up with it. After the mid-1960s, Winnipeg's economy started to falter.

The R & H Agencies building at 175 Donald Street in downtown Winnipeg was a beehive of activity during the 1960s. It was a really old house built on about a 30-foot-wide lot. The front of the main floor contained the office, where real estate clients could negotiate, write, or accept offers. At the back of the main floor was a rolling machine on which Rubin and/or Harry rolled long lengths of chamois in spare moments onto cardboard tubes so that they could be shipped to the coat manufacturers of the east coast. This was hard physical work. Both arms stretched the chamois with all their might, keeping both edges straight, while the shoulders heaved the machine so that it would roll in a circle. The larger the roll became, the heavier the work. The back door hall did double duty as a shipping and delivery room. An unfinished basement was the storage area for chamois scraps. The second floor of the building contained sewing machines for contract sewers who did not have their own machines. Also on the second floor, chamois was cut into rectangles and packaged in plastic see-through bags. Rehydrated and then dried sponges were also packaged there. The attic, effectively a third floor, was where the compressed sponges were soaked in water tubs to expand to their original shapes and then laid out on nets to dry. Nets were hung from every corner of the attic; it was like going into a small fishing village in the middle of downtown Winnipeg.

After a few years of doing absolutely everything themselves, Rubin and Harry began to hire people here and there, first a receptionist who could also sew, then a strong lad to stretch the chamois onto rolls. Harry got married in 1961 to a

Winnipeg Jewish woman, Doris Zalik. She was a very clever woman, and a few years after she and Harry were married she was asked to contribute to the business by doing the paperwork and books, answering phones, and so on. She started working in the business part time. Other family members worked too. Even I worked there at least one summer as a child stretching the scraps of chamois so that they could more easily be sewn. I went from one seamstress to the next stretching and smoothing the piles of unsewn scraps. I remember that the radio was always on, and I learned all the top tunes. I'm pretty sure now that I was more a hindrance than a help, but my father paid me for my work. Aside from my hourly wage, some days he would take me to the local café, a greasy spoon, for lunch. It was a pleasure for me to be working with my father in the summers. I was only 10 years old in the summer of 1965, but he made me feel like I was really useful. I remember my favourite tune, "I Got You Babe," playing on the radio. Watching all the activity in the Donald Street building, seeing my father work, I was sure that the kind of frenzied pace of work that Harry and Rubin kept up was normal, that everyone worked like they did. Now I know differently.

In those days, my father worked very long hours. For six days a week, he would leave for the office before I awoke in the morning for school and return home after I had gone to bed. On some nights, I would make myself stay awake waiting for him to get home. When he came home, he would check to see whether we children were still awake to give us a goodnight kiss even before he would eat dinner. There was not much that my mother could do to keep his food warm without drying it out. His dinner was therefore always cold by the time he got home, so he might tell us a story in bed while he waited until the food was reheated (there were no microwaves then).

Sometimes reheating would burn the food, but he ate it without complaint. If my mother had waited until he was home to cook his meal, then my father would have had it for breakfast.

On Sundays, he would stay home and play with us. In the summers, we always played catch in the backyard with a rubber ball; I had a baseball glove, and he used his bare hands. Sundays were his special pleasure, the only day of the week that we would be together as a family. We children came to appreciate Sundays as much as he did. Sunday night we might go to the kosher deli near my grandmother's house and take out corned beef and coleslaw, and my mother would make a deli-style dinner, my favourite at the time. Sometimes we would join my uncle Sam and his family at their Sunday-night ritual of Chinese food in Winnipeg's "Chinatown," consisting of two Chinese restaurants across the road from each other. In the winter on Sunday afternoons, we would stay home or visit with friends or relatives. In the summer, though, my father would love to take us for drives in the country or to a lake. In Winnipeg, summer lasts about 10 weeks, so everyone takes advantage of as much of it as they can.

Saturday nights, conversely, belonged to my mother. She had a good friend, Rose Bogach, whom she adored. My parents got together every Saturday night with Rose and her husband, Nate, and they went out to eat at Rae and Jerry's Steak House on Portage Avenue. Every Saturday night my father would order a big meal and come home with indigestion from having eaten too much. He knew that he would be sick, yet he enjoyed it too much to stop himself from eating. I would hear him groaning in the middle of the night from a stomach ache. Overeating was his one personal indulgence throughout his postwar life, and I for one can certainly understand that. He had been hungry all the time for years, and now he let himself eat as much as he wanted.

Rubin's sister Chasia moved to Winnipeg in 1954. She and her husband had immigrated to Canada in 1951 and lived originally in Montreal. Her husband was quite different from her, and they separated in 1954 before I was born. Naturally, Chasia took comfort in being near her brother. Harry was still in Montreal at the time and not yet married, so my parents offered to have Chasia live with them in their little house on Seven Oaks Avenue. Newly separated, Chasia lived with our family for a year. She had her own room in the attic of the house.

Chasia helped my mother to care for three-year-old Helen and for the new baby, me. My mother was particularly tolerant of Chasia, but a year of having her in the house was a lot to ask. There was room in the family for only one woman of the house, and this was my mother's house. Chasia realized at the appropriate time that she had better find her own place. She moved out but kept close, and a few years later she worked with her brothers at the chamois factory. In their business in those days, anyone willing to work was welcome, especially family members. It just meant that the business would have to generate more money to sustain them all. It did, though we lived very modestly. Only when I had grown up did I realize just how modestly we had lived and how we all had been satisfied with very little. We considered ourselves middle class. We were middle class in the way that we lived but probably not in the little amount of spending that we did. Of course, my parents wasted no money on vices such as alcohol, we didn't take expensive trips, and when we did go out to eat at the Chinese restaurants with our cousins I suspect that my uncle Sam paid. But we were happy.

In 1962, my grandmother Fanny, who had been living alone in her house on Seven Oaks Avenue since her husband's death in 1957, had a debilitating stroke. She was unable to do anything without assistance, not being able to move her left side. My parents took her in for six months while she was learning to walk again with a walker (which she did not accomplish) and learning to cope with her disability. My grandmother never recovered but did move back to her home with the assistance of around-the-clock care. My mother took care of her while she lived at our house, but it was my father who welcomed her to stay with us for as long as she did.

From this time on for the rest of his life, my father was overweight. He never bought in to the healthy habits of keeping his weight reasonable. He had promised himself in 1942 that if he survived the war he would never again know the feeling of hunger. We children chided him countless times for the bowling ball on his stomach out of genuine concern for his health, but he always replied good naturedly that he had lived for a long time with a big stomach, and if he lived a few more years with it he'd be happy. It was hard for me to accept that my father was so easily prepared to forsake his health for the pleasures of the flesh (eating without restraint), and I tried to convince him that he could eat plenty, just not food that was so fattening. But he liked the taste, and he didn't want to exercise self-control when it came to eating. Who am I to judge that behaviour? He had gone through hunger that thankfully most people will never know, and that had to have affected him, as the sheer hell of the Holocaust affected all its survivors. The scars left on my father were relatively mild, and I have to be thankful for that. Others had much deeper psychological wounds.

In 1965, our family received an invitation to the bar mitzvah of Lou Bzrezinski, the son of Pola, the cousin with whom my father had grown up and spent years with in the Polish forests. He decided that this was an important enough event that he would take the whole family to Montreal. We went by train from Winnipeg to Montreal and returned by plane. All five of us and Chasia went to Montreal, and it was a wonderful reunion. The bar mitzvah was a big success, and we children got to see first-hand how important the cousins were to our father, people whom he had not seen in almost 20 years and whom we, his children and his wife, had never met. I suppose that most people remember the first big trip in their lives. This trip was for the purpose of celebrating a special occasion with cousins. We spent all the time with them and remembered this aspect of the family connection of this trip all our lives. It probably shaped our lives forever.

By the mid-1960s, the R & H Agencies building kept getting fuller and busier. In 1966, my father told me that he had the best year of his life in business. He made $10,000 before taxes. Although this was not a lot of money in those days for most people, it was two-thirds of the price that he'd paid ten years before for our house on the last residential street on the north side of Winnipeg. To him, it was a great deal of money. I was so proud of him. I could see that hard work was paying off. My father and uncle Harry were also following their plan and amassing little bits of land here and there, 10 percent of a piece of bare land to the east of Winnipeg, 15 percent of a farm to the north, and so on. Over the years, many of these parcels were sold at little or no profit after carrying costs were taken into account. My father still held some of the pieces after 35 years, and he passed away in 2001 with a couple still in his estate. In 2015, 55 years after its purchase, his heirs sold off the last piece of land. The value, as I said, did not appreciate for almost 50 years. Sometimes I think about what could have been if he had bought those properties in the 1960s in Vancouver, Calgary, or Toronto. But my father chose not to think that way. If he did think about it later, he never expressed regret.

By 1967, the little house on Donald Street was becoming overcrowded, with too many bosses and not enough employees. Things were testy and carried on to arguments between Rubin and Harry. In 1968, they knew that it was not going to work anymore. Harry offered to buy out Rubin's portion of the business. Without having a clue about what he would do for a living, Rubin accepted Harry's offer.

CHAPTER 13

The Valley

The brothers had a quick closing. Neither one wanted things to become worse between them, and they wanted to stay friends. The price must have been a good compromise; neither was that happy about the price, but neither complained about it. My father was in a position all of a sudden of having no idea what business to enter. Neither did he have a lot of money with which to buy a business. He didn't want to compete with his brother in any of the businesses that he had sold; maybe that had been part of the agreement between them, but I didn't know at the time to ask. He decided that at age 44 he would have to start something entirely new.

After looking around and investigating various opportunities, my father decided that he wanted to become a hotelier. Not a Hyatt-type hotelier, for he knew that he could not afford the price of a fancy hotel. He also was not interested in a motel, which in Winnipeg had a short busy season but was quiet the rest of the year, and he would have been bored to tears. No, the type of hotel that would give him lots of work year-round (and he knew that if he worked hard he could make a good living) was a skid row hotel that made most of its profits from beer sales. For over a year, my father looked at hotels in Winnipeg, mostly on Main Street near downtown. But he didn't have enough money to buy even those hotels. They were lucrative businesses, and their owners knew it. Any hotel for sale was going for a hefty price. Most were not for sale at all. My father made offers to the maximum extent of his credit and capital, but they were not enough. Still, his mind was made up. If the owners of the hotels were driving such a hard bargain, then a hotel must be as good or a better business than he had thought. Unfortunately, his offers were rejected time after time. Four months went by, then six months. He would look at another hotel, try to structure a deal, make his best offer, and get refused. Most times he worked and worked on structuring a viable offer but in the end was unable to give potential sellers what they wanted. Eight months went by, then ten months. My father's mood was getting worse and worse. A man who had worked night and day to make life for his family better, who thought that he had to earn a living to provide for his family, cannot sit idly by while his living expenses are eating into his capital. It was another one of the hard things that he had to face in his life, at least emotionally, and it was getting to him.

An aspect of his depressed state was the reappearance of nightmares that my father had not had since 1953. He would awaken in the night dreaming that he was back in the forests of Poland or in the ghetto with his parents and little sister. He would try to warn them that they had to flee the ghetto and try to live in the forests, but for some reason they could not hear him. He would awaken with a jolt, sweating and heart pounding. He had subconsciously or perhaps consciously suppressed thinking about the worst aspects of the war for so long. The memories were coming out now that he had other worries to compound his anxiety. This period was the only time that my father often remembered the war and the atrocities that it held for him.

After a fruitless year, my father started to look farther afield. A skid row hotel was for sale in Regina for a price that he could afford. It was still most of his money, but the profits were good for an owner/operator prepared to work hard. He was certainly prepared for that. He discussed moving the family from Winnipeg. He told my mother that there was little choice, that he had to start making a living. She was very reluctant to leave Winnipeg for a number of reasons: she knew no one in Regina; she had lived all her life in Winnipeg, and all her friends and relatives were there; and her mother, who had not recovered the use of her left side after her stroke in 1962, was very dependent on her only daughter. Since Fanny had left our house six months after her stroke, my mother went to her home every day, visiting and supervising the care aides.

If my mother left Winnipeg, then Fanny probably would have to be placed in a nursing home. Uncle Sam could not dedicate the kind of time that my mother could to their mother; he was a busy businessman with his own young children. Understandably, Fanny had always raged against moving to a nursing home. As long as she was at home, in theory she maintained some autonomy in her life, even if in reality she had little. Everything was done for her, and her finances were managed by her children. Yet my mother knew that she had to give my father the opportunity to succeed. Perhaps if he had found the hotel in Regina after only a couple of months of unemployment she would have said no, but after seeing how much he suffered during the almost 17 months that he did not work she knew that she had no choice. She agreed to move.

There were also other factors at play in my family's life at that time. Sam had been diagnosed with Parkinson's disease in 1967. He was a relatively young man to have contracted the disease, only 47. In 1967, Parkinson's was a quick way to complete body breakdown and death. When his doctor suggested that he join a trial for a new experimental drug called L-dopa being carried out in Minneapolis, 600 kilometres away, Sam agreed. He started making frequent trips to Minneapolis to be treated. He obviously had less time for his mother and less time for his business and family than he had before the diagnosis. He ended up being lucky to be chosen for L-dopa's initial trials. Thirty years later L-dopa was still used as the main retardant for the progression of Parkinson's. It probably gave Sam a life span of 10–15 years more than he otherwise would have had. Because of his illness, it was doubly hard for my mother to leave him too.

In the end, they kept their mother at home with around-the-clock care, Sam and his wife, Ann, going as often as they could, and my mother visiting from Regina frequently. As it turned out, Fanny passed away about 18 months after my mother left Winnipeg.

CHAPTER 14

Regina

My father closed the deal on the hotel in January 1970. In the weeks just before the purchase, he took my mother on a two-week vacation to Hawaii. He knew that after the purchase of the hotel he would have few holidays for years to come. They went to Hawaii with Rose and Nate Bogach. Sam and Ann Moser were also in Hawaii at that time. My parents had the time of their lives. They let loose, walked on the beach every day, enjoyed the wonderful weather. For my father, the excitement of the impending purchase and the mix of sun, beach, and palm trees gave him the feeling that he had reached a piece of heaven. He could not believe the beauty. That holiday and the knowledge of having a demanding career awaiting him brought him back in all his vigour.

The rest of the family, me included, were not happy about moving to Regina. All our friends were in Winnipeg. Other than my father, our family didn't move until later in June when the school year was finished. It would have been too disruptive to take us out of school before then. By the time we moved at the end of June 1970, everything was set. We even had a very nice house to move into. My father had surprised us all, especially my mother, by buying a house in a nice area of Regina that only he had seen. We all had to admit that it was a lot better than our house in Winnipeg. House prices in Regina were cheap then compared with those in Winnipeg. My father wanted this move to Regina to be one with which we all would be happy. He also wanted us to believe that there would be tangible results from his hard work. The house was luxurious compared with what we were used to.

Helen was 18 in 1970, and she was heavily involved in the hippy/radical/communist/free spirit movement. She moved to Regina with the family, but she moved straight into a commune. She took part in organized marches and lived with people whose politics were left wing or more radical. It was the age of rebellion, and Helen certainly did rebel. I was on the periphery of those politics as well. I knew how to walk the walk and talk the talk, but I wasn't entirely convinced of the righteousness of all leftist politics. My ideas were not an embarrassment for Helen; I didn't debate the issues very often with her friends when they spouted dogma. Besides, I wasn't quite old enough that my ideas mattered to her crowd. So I was welcomed, and I wore my hair long and frizzy, and I sometimes marched with them, sometimes didn't. It was the best of both worlds. I could live on the edge of rebellion, but I lived at home and ate at my parents' table. Helen didn't.

She had some major clashes with our parents at that time. Our father could not be against his daughter; it wasn't in his heart. He also could not be against his wife, for the sake of peace in the house. Our mother was totally against Helen's lifestyle and let Helen know. She was always welcome at the house, but some of her friends were not. She stayed away from our home more often than not. After a few months, perhaps half a year of living in Regina, Helen moved back to Winnipeg. Her anti-establishment phase ran its course, and she soon enrolled at the University of Manitoba.

My telling of this part of Helen's life is not meant to belittle her ideals and her way of life in any way. It was the early 1970s, and my sister was part of a movement that she believed in completely. She kept some of the ideas that she had about politics and all her aspirations for feminism for many years. Feminism became and remained a major force in her life and politics. Over time, the hard edge of her politics softened, her views became less revolutionary, and she entered the mainstream. Before Helen was finished being a revolutionary, however, she made her mark as a feminist. In 1975, as one of five female students in the 120-student Faculty of Law at the University of Manitoba, she led the women into the men's only locker room so that women too would have rights to lockers. Until then, there was a locker room for men but none for women. Helen took part in countless women's groups and forums. She took me into the political fray, too, and I marched with her whenever I could. She was right about most things. She softened, the mainstream became more liberal, and mainstream politics and her politics eventually merged.

My parents lived in Regina from 1970 to 1977. It was a good time for them. My father worked hard, but he loved to work hard. He earned more than he ever had before and was the boss of a hotel. He was even referred to as "boss." There were at least 20 employees of the hotel, including front desk staff, chamber maids, beer parlour servers, managers, and cleaners. There was a coffee shop at the hotel that he rented out to a Chinese couple, a rare minority in Regina in the early 1970s. My father was back to working six days a week for 12 to 16 hours a day. He would generally get up at 9 a.m. and eat breakfast with my mother. He would get to the hotel at about 10. There he would count the cash from the night before and do the banking. The beer parlour opened at 11, and he would make sure that it was opened properly, that there was sufficient staff, inventory, change, et cetera. The staff were not very reliable, and my father always had to be ready either to do the job himself or to call for standby staff. He was on excellent terms with most of his customers, perhaps 40 percent Caucasian and 60 percent Indigenous. Those who showed initiative would almost always be offered jobs, starting as fill-in staff and, if they worked well, moving to full-time positions. My father showed colour blindness in this respect, for he would befriend people and offer them positions without regard for race or colour or gender. For this, he was respected, and when there was trouble at the beer parlour, and there often was just because of the nature of the clientele, his intervention would usually end it.

My father spent early afternoons on administration and ordering. The hotel had been built in the 1920s and was in constant need of repair. He would find handymen or offer jobs to handy people whom he met in his bar and get things fixed, after a fashion. Because handiwork was not his strong suit, he sometimes could not tell if something was properly fixed or not. He did not deal with companies in the yellow pages that gave 90-day written guarantees. If the next day the problem arose again that he had paid to have fixed the day before, then he would simply hire another "handyman" whom he found and try again. He was sometimes able to pay the workers for casual jobs in free beer rather than cash. His cost for the beer was much less than the cost for his customers, so he thought that he was getting a bargain. My father could never resist a bargain.

At a minimum on Thursdays to Saturdays, and on other days when welfare cheques were distributed, my father would stay at the hotel in the late afternoon to be in the beer parlour when the business became heavy. His main purpose was to ensure that his employees, specifically the bartenders, did not steal too much. In those days, the methods for counting inventory were primitive, and my father didn't use all of those methods anyway. He knew that the employees were stealing a certain amount from him, and he accepted it as part of the business. As long as he was making a living, he could live with a bit of stealing. If he were present at the beer parlour, either the employees would take less because they would be afraid of getting caught, or he could watch the braver employees to see what was going on and get rid of the worst offenders. This system more or less worked as his inventory system. The beer parlour was busy on these nights, and sales were all in cash. Theft could occur by the employees drinking the liquor, taking the liquor home, keeping the customers' payments for themselves, or taking cash from the till by ringing in the wrong amounts. It all went on.

On most Mondays to Wednesdays, the beer parlour (the upgraded word since those days is *lounge*, I suppose, but to me the term "beer parlour" best described it) was less busy, and my father often came home for dinner around 6 p.m. He would arrive to eat with us and then go back to work about 8 or 8:30 p.m. He would be home on those days for two to three hours. The beer parlour would close at 1 a.m., and he would coax or chase out the stragglers, making sure that the cash was safely in his vault, letting in the cleaners, and getting home about 1:45 a.m. It took only 10 minutes to drive from the hotel to our house at that time of night, even though we lived on the outskirts of the city. After we had been in Regina for a few years, my father would also take the odd Friday night off or Saturday until 9 or 10 p.m. if there was a special occasion or a reason to be home or out with us. At times, we felt absolutely spoiled with how much we got to see him. He had some of the family working at the hotel too. We were clerks at the front desk. I was full time in the summer and on Saturdays during the winter for the two years that I lived there. My mother would fill in sometimes when the regular desk clerk didn't show up. Helen and Max worked there much less. Helen was not in Regina after six months, and Max was too young at the time. But we also dropped by the hotel to see our father or to pick things up most times that we went downtown. He often brought home treats from the hotel, especially chocolates and packaged chips. Our mother had a strong sweet tooth (which I inherited) and had pantries full of junk food at home. We were living pretty well.

After they had been in Regina about four years, my father could see that things were not going well for his sister, Chasia, in Winnipeg. She was out of work, and she missed being close to my parents. He thought that she would be better off near him in Regina. He invited her to come to Regina, and he would find her a job. She agreed to come but somehow could not get packed up and make the move. This went on for months—Chasia didn't have the energy to pack and leave, yet she was unemployed and miserable. One weekend my father simply hopped on a plane, packed up what he thought his sister needed, and threw out or gave away the rest. He took her and her things on the plane and brought her to Regina. He brought her in a matter of two days. He gave her a job at the hotel, and she was part of their lives once again on a daily basis. My mother introduced Chasia to the Jewish community, and she ended up living in Regina until after my parents moved away in 1977.

My mother had some of the happiest times of her life in Regina. She made several good friends and became active in the Jewish community. The community was very small and needed and encouraged everyone to participate. She joined the synagogue sisterhood and B'nai B'rith women and Hadassah, and she was never lonely. If my mother wanted to see my father when he was at work, then she drove downtown to the hotel in 15 minutes and saw him. He could make himself available to us at almost any time of day (late evenings and nights were the problem, but we didn't go there much at night). My mother also had an experience in Regina that had never happened to her before: she was not in anyone's shadow. She was not her mother's daughter or Sam's little sister; she was her own person. She could be herself, and she was doing well at it. She had always felt somewhat inadequate beside her smart and successful brother, his capable wife, her exceedingly bright cousins, and her overprotective parents. It was not really their fault, it was her reaction to their traits, even though they loved her very much. In Regina, no one knew her brother or her parents, they knew only her and her husband, and they accepted and liked these newcomers. My mother felt great.

For six years in Regina, my parents lived what could be called the good life. True, it was distasteful that my father's hotel was a place for alcoholics to drink themselves to ruin. This was the one serious blot. But my father was successful at keeping his business humming and had less than his fair share of trouble considering that it was a skid row hotel, and I believe that was because of how he treated people equally and with dignity. That didn't mean that there wasn't trouble from time to time. One drunk would get mad at another, and all the onlookers would take sides. They would forget where they were and start to fight. Sometimes a pool cue would be swung, and rarely a knife would be opened. Once every month or so the police would be called to break up a fight or charge someone with assault. My father was never touched. He solved most of the problems with the smile on his face and his calming words.

Near the end, though, he started to get tired of it. In 1976, he was 51 years old, and the pace was starting to get to him. He wisely started to take more time off and just didn't let it bother him as much that the employees would likely steal more while he was away. He started to think that sometime in the foreseeable future he would sell the hotel. But he didn't foresee that his business would end as abruptly as it did.

On May 22, 1976, in the early morning hours, the Met Hotel burned down. The front page of the Saturday Regina *Leader-Post* had a quarter-page picture of the hotel burning with the caption "Fire Damage High at Met Hotel." The newspaper reported no injuries among the guests. "The first call from the Met Hotel (at about 2:30 a.m.) was unclear, and by the time the firemen arrived flames were shooting from five windows on the top floor," said Regina's deputy fire chief. It was determined later that the fire had been started by a smoker falling asleep with a cigarette in his hand. The hotel was not burned to the ground, but the replacement cost was higher than the value of the insurance. My father was again out of work. He had some paperwork and lots of legal hassles in getting the insurance money. He also had to tear down the hotel structure (it was a hazard) in order to sell the empty lot. The sale of the lot was not hard. It was right across from the police station, and the city was keen to expand the police facilities. My father was quick to accept the city's offer. He complained several times that unfortunately he did not have the hotel insured for enough, that it was worth more than the insurance company ended up paying. He haggled for a while with the insurance company but not for long. By late 1976, he needed something else to do.

CHAPTER 15

Vancouver

Although they had enjoyed Regina, like most Canadians my parents were drawn to the climate of the West Coast. In fact, they had another strong draw in that Helen, who had now finished law school and done well, had decided to move to Vancouver. A person who graduates from law school must spend time learning the profession with an established lawyer in order to qualify to practise law in Canada, a process called articling. Helen found employment as an articling student in Vancouver during the summer of 1976. My father had looked at several businesses in Regina, but none had much appeal to him. He was not going to become involved with a hotel again, at least the kind that he had owned, and other businesses that he looked at seemed to be too small time, such as a Subway franchise or a clothing retail store with some of his Regina friends. He couldn't really see himself as a retailer in Regina. My parents decided to sell the house and make the big move to Vancouver. They didn't seriously consider moving back to Winnipeg, for that was their past. In the spring of 1977, they moved not only to Vancouver but to the affluent west side.

My parents didn't know much about Vancouver; in fact, they knew no one in the city except their daughter and her boyfriend. They knew, though, that they wanted to live in a Jewish area of the city. Vancouver at the time had half as many Jews as Winnipeg, but they thought that the "Jewish area" would be similar. Their home from 1956 to 1970 on Royal Crescent in Winnipeg was on a street that had Jewish families in 32 of 36 homes. Surrounding areas were not quite as ghettoized, but to my parents a Jewish area meant that there were quite a few Jewish families on each street. Not so in Vancouver. Any area that had as many as two Jewish families on a block was considered by realtors a Jewish area if that was what one was searching for. Jews in Vancouver thought so too. And to some extent the realtors were right, for few places in Vancouver were more densely Jewish than a few houses on one block. The Jewish community was spread out in Vancouver, very different from that in Winnipeg.

My parents bought a house on 64th Avenue near Cambie Street, not in the heart of the Jewish area but close enough, considering the price that they were prepared to pay. They had sold a split-level modern home in Regina and bought a much older and smaller one-storey and basement home in Vancouver, and they had paid four times as much for the Vancouver home as they had received in proceeds for the Regina home. That was the way things were in Vancouver and continue to be, but my parents were not quite ready for it then, and it came as a shock. Yet they had purchased the house because things had been good in Regina, they thought they were in reasonably good shape financially, and my father surely would be earning money again soon.

During the first six months that he was in Vancouver, he tried a variety of businesses. He looked at motels and hotels, but most were out of his league pricewise. The reasons that had kept him out of the Winnipeg hotel market in 1969 applied in the Vancouver hotel market, even though he had more money now to purchase one. Vancouver prices for real estate-based businesses were sky high compared with what he was used to, especially compared with prices on the Prairies. As he continued to look, my father began to realize that the savings he had accumulated in Regina were not going to last as long as he had hoped, nor would they buy him the kind of business that he would have been able to buy in Regina. He started looking at businesses that did not involve the purchase of real estate, even though real estate was his primary interest. Since leaving Mid-West Garments in 1960, he had always thought that, if he could accumulate and eventually pay off real estate, he would do well. "A man must own land!" as Woody Allen so cleverly mimicked in the movie *Love and Death*. He might have been mimicking my father.

He tried his hand at a plant store. He (and Helen in her spare time) would stand outside his store on the sidewalk during the summer of 1977 hawking plants and flowers at two dollars or so per pot. Every customer had to learn about a variety of plants first before committing those two dollars, whether the plant likes sun or shade, when to plant it, which other plants go well with it, when it will bloom, and so on. It was a big investment of time for a mere two dollars. Now, don't get me wrong, my father loved plants and gardening. Gardening was his only hobby, and he always had a garden when he lived in Winnipeg and Regina, and various hardy vegetables always grew even though he was able to dedicate only a few precious hours to them on Sunday mornings. Back then, at the height of the long summer days when the sunset was late and true darkness did not come until well after 10 p.m., he would get home in time to spend a few minutes in the garden while my mother was warming his dinner. My father drew from his years in the forest to guess how certain plants would react now that they were in a domestic setting. He was seldom off the mark.

His love of plants, however, was not enough to sustain his interest in a business in which he had to expend considerable effort, time, and expertise to bring in each two dollars, especially when he had to think first about the inventory and rent and all other expenses. Especially, too, when he had just left a business in which the two-dollar payments were streaming in through waiters and waitresses and bartenders and in which he was the conductor of a finely tuned beer-selling symphony. My father was not ready to go back to being the lead violin without a backup orchestra. If this metaphor doesn't work for you, you still get the idea.

My father packed up the plant business and looked into other things. Nothing seemed to be right. Then he was introduced by a real estate agent to an Ismaili family looking for a partner for their leather coat business. They were not asking a lot for the half share, but they wanted the investor to equal their shareholder loans. In other words, pay them something and inject some capital into the business. For the purpose of anonymity, I will call the business True Fashion Leather Limited (TFL), which had annual revenues in 1976 of about $3 million. There were over 40 employees, including sewers, shippers, salespeople, accounting clerks, shop supervisors, cutters, buyers, and designers. Now here was a business that my father could relate to, the *shmata* business. Sales were mostly to American buyers, including well-known retail clothing chains. The factory was about 20,000 square feet (1,858 square metres) of a building in Gastown. The remainder of the building was occupied by Koret, a manufacturer of women's low-priced fashion clothing. Koret was managed by some Jewish people, though not owned by them, and TFL even did some contract sewing work for Koret when leather orders were slow. This all appealed greatly to my father. He quickly purchased the half share and became a co-president of the company at an annual salary of $42,000. He was to manage the company with the other co-president.

His partners in the venture were charming. His co-president, whom I will call Amir, was about 10 years younger than my father but had been in business all his life. The family, whom I will call the Kassams, did everything together, and everything was business, business, business; they were very entrepreneurial. Amir's father had somehow brought a lot of money out of Uganda and was prepared to back his three sons in their entrepreneurial ventures when the risks were not too high. The first son had bought and was managing a well-known motel and restaurant in a close suburb of Vancouver. The second son was Amir. The third son (whom I'll call Mehbob) was a wheeler-dealer, flying all around Canada and the United States in search of a deal. He would find a deal, tie it up with an interim purchase agreement, line up financing and partners, and then take a piece of the action if not the majority of it. Mehbob did find good deals, but he always made them better with the following tactic: at the closing table, when the sellers were ready to sign and get their money, the legal documents had been prepared, and the cheques were ready for payment, Mehbob would suddenly demand concessions beyond what had been agreed to and stated in the documents. He would almost always get at least a portion of what he wanted. Very few sellers of businesses who have placed, if not spent, the money that they would get on closing day would walk away from a deal on the basis of a last-minute issue unless it was a big issue. Mehbob was a master. More than once he walked away from a deal if he did not get his way. He sensed how hard he could push potential sellers. Some were more anxious than others. At some point, most of the sellers, especially those who were tired of the business or had immediate holiday plans, would say screw it, give him what he wants, and finish the deal. A minority did not. The advantage was that his word was not his bond. Mehbob used his verbal agreements with others against them and wouldn't live up to those agreements. If they didn't like it, then they could sue his purchasing company. In the commercial world, businesspeople know how much of a hassle litigation is in terms of time and costs. Besides, Mehbob usually tied up the deal in a newly incorporated company that had few if any assets to seize if a judgment was rendered against it.

I had to hand it to Mehbob. He would lie awake at night and try to think of ways to get more out of the other side on every transaction—at least that is what he confided to me once. He would also solicit the participation of his brothers and father in this pursuit. He was very bright and took advantage of every situation. In the years since I knew him, I heard talk that he made fortunes and lost them and perhaps made them again. Mehbob with his scheming mind was partly who became my father's business partner. He wasn't supposed to be part of the deal; Amir was officially the partner. But the Kassam half of TFL was owned through a family holding company, so each of the Kassams could claim that he had an interest in being in the office and checking things out. Worse, Mehbob did not have an office for his own business dealings, so he spent a lot of time using TFL facilities.

Before my father bought in to the business, Mehbob had always used the TFL office as his personal office for supplies, secretarial work, and long-distance calls when he was in town. In fact, so did his father. When my father bought in, he expected that the practice would cease. It did not. He was the newcomer and a gentle soul and was not prepared to rock the boat. To some extent, he enjoyed having them around, discussing business deals, and getting advice on the leather business. Even when my father thought that they overstayed their welcome, he was not prepared to confront his partners over their personal use of TFL facilities. The expenses were not a lot on their own, but they did add up. Mehbob tried to convince my father, and did convince him for a while, that it was beneficial to have him around so that my father might be the first to get an opportunity to invest in his deals. Mehbob was at TFL perhaps 10 days a month and his father half that number. They occasionally paid for their long-distance calls. Amir would buy them lunch on the company account when my father was with them, and he knew that it happened when he wasn't present too. And, yes, it bothered him. They were eating into his half of the profits.

I am getting ahead of myself. I have described the character of the people with whom my father had become partners to indicate that he was in a new league, one that he had not played in before. This would end up causing him trouble.

At the beginning, though, my father was happy. He was earning a decent living according to his standards. Even though $42,000 in 1977–80 was not a great deal of money, the needs of my parents were not that great. They had paid for their house, and they were not extravagant people or world travellers. My father was a manager, with over 40 people calling him "boss." He dealt with large financial numbers (for him) and went on important business lunches with colleagues, partners, buyers, suppliers, and bankers. He was close to lots of action with Mehbob telling him of the business deals that he was cooking up (with embellishments or omissions that suited his purposes). At the beginning, my father was very happy.

When he was happy, he was one of the most positive people whom one could meet. The 1970s were a long period of happiness and optimism for my father. One time when I was visiting Vancouver in my early 20s before I moved there, he picked me up at the airport in his late-model car, and I was impressed. I said that things were good for our family and for most of Canada, and even then—thinking about emerging environmental problems and the economic downturn that was predicted—I said that things were so good that they probably would get worse. My father was shocked and totally disagreed with me: especially for our family, but also for the world, things would not get worse, and all our lives would get better and better. He was so convinced, he was so sure, that I believed him.

During the first couple of years of owning TFL, my father travelled to Japan, Hong Kong, Singapore, and Bangkok, partly with government funds aimed to encourage manufacturers to export to East Asia. My parents had a wonderful time. It was part holiday, part business. Of course, my father had no clue about business ways in Asia, and the business side of the trip was not very successful. He tried to get the sales in Asia that he had told the government trade officials that he was after, but he didn't get many sales. That was no reflection just on him, for at that time most Canadian businesspeople had no idea how to conduct business in Asia. But he was satisfied with the trip, and he had seen a new part of the world. Those were the Pierre Trudeau years when the government was prepared to spend a lot of money to diversify Canada's economy away from that of the United States. The whole government initiative failed, and Canada's economy was much more closely tied to that of the United States 15 years later than it was previously. Soon after those trips, Asia's clothing manufacturers took over pretty much all that business worldwide.

In 1978, my parents and my brother, Max, made their first trip to Israel. It was something that my father had been looking forward to for decades. Now he thought that he could afford to go in style. He wore a beautiful full-length leather coat that he had made in his factory to keep him warm in case it was cool. They arrived in Israel and hired a car and driver, not because the public tours wouldn't take him to the tourist and holy sites that he wanted to see, but because the tours wouldn't take him to his *lantzmen*, his fellow "townspeople" from Gzetl. He spent a lot of time finding the addresses of all the *lantzmen* and relatives whom he could think of, most of whom he had never met, and he just went to their homes. He was delighted to see them all, and in one *moshav* ("communal farm") where he met a *lantzman* who gave him a particularly warm welcome, he took his full-length leather coat off and gave it to the startled Israeli as a gift. These relatives and *lantzmen* meant the world to my father.

In the late 1970s, too, he did a repeat of what he had done for Chasia about five years prior. She was alone in Regina, with the idea that she might follow my parents to Vancouver after they were settled there. She was not able to pack and move herself, so my father went back to Regina one weekend, packed her up, and brought her to Vancouver. She spent her whole life near him, except for the five years after Harry and Rubin arrived in Canada. Chasia was part of our Vancouver family life weekly, coming to dinners on Fridays and keeping in touch with my parents daily. Although she was stubborn and hard to take at times, there was a closeness between her and my father that lasted all their lives. Chasia became a resident of the Louis Brier Home and Hospital in 1992 and died there in 2000. During her time in Vancouver, everyone in our immediate family visited her at least weekly.

My father was able during his first couple of years at TFL to enlarge his house on 64th Avenue, with contractors who normally worked for the business. I expect that he got a pretty fair deal from the contractors for the work on his house when they did so much work for his business. His partners did business the same way.

What my father did not realize during this time was that he would have difficulties both in his relations with his partners and in the operations of the business. I have described the nature of his partners. Because he was essentially a decent businessman, he was better off with respect to the business itself than he was in his relations with his partners. Although as an immigrant in his mid-50s he was not quite keeping up with the fast-paced world of fashion, at TFL he didn't really have to know about fashion: the company had hired a full-time fashion designer. The designer was an ex-Israeli whom my father thought that he could deal with since they had their love of Israel in common. Boy, was he wrong! The designer was very temperamental, throwing tantrums like a child and causing life to be miserable for the TFL owners. The designer had always designed a line that could sell, however, and he did it in time (barely) for the line to be produced for the selling season. It was difficult to put up with the designer, but my father had no one else. Later, when he owned the factory alone (yes, I'll get to that), he tried to bring in a designer from eastern Canada to produce the line instead of the Israeli. The Israeli designer had a fit when he heard that he might be replaced and somehow put the Fear of God into the easterner, who abruptly cut off discussions. TFL was stuck with its temperamental Israeli-born designer.

TFL's owners had hired staff to operate the production side and a production manager. My father managed the production manager but not the production itself. On the accounting side, my father could read numbers and understand instinctively where cuts could and should be made, which expenditures were necessary, and how to increase profits. Sales were handled by sales staff and a sales manager who could talk the lingo of high fashion. My father could and would cut a deal with buyers when the sale was close, and the sales staff needed the hand of management to close the deal. In business, one of the most important aspects is the management of employees. My father handled this task well. The employees liked him and respected him.

TFL was a manufacturer that sold to retail outlets and wholesalers. It manufactured leather jackets and coats, not high fashion but including bomber jackets, regular-length jackets, and full-length coats for men and women. The market segment was lower to mid-market leather, competing more on the price than on the latest fashion.

In 1980, the economy of the United States was starting to falter. Interest rates were rising to unprecedented levels, and retail sales were slowing down. Some American retail chains were experiencing troubles. One of TFL's largest customers, which owed TFL in excess of $180,000, was considering creditor protection in bankruptcy and was in the process of making a proposal to creditors. The chain still purchased from TFL but was purchasing much less than previously and had to do so on a cash basis. TFL was very thinly capitalized, and $180,000 represented almost all the shareholder equity and more than all the profits for the company for the year, including salaries for managers. My father was not aware of the extent of the problem. He was optimistic and thought that the retail chain would work out its problems. No one in 1980 believed that interest rates would go as high as they did. In August 1981, the prime lending rate reached an all-time high of 22.75 percent in Canada.

There were other troubles for TFL too. The Israeli designer was causing more problems than before. Contracting work for Koret in the slow leather season was lessening for the same reasons that retailers were hurting. As well, the building lease of TFL's manufacturing facility was coming due in about 18 months, and the company had to plan a major move, for Koret was going to expand and take over the whole building. It was no easy feat to move the company's operations. The new facility had to be planned for clothing manufacturing, with proper facilities for the dozens of cutting and sewing machines, administration, a showroom, a shipping room, access to rail, trucking, and so on. There were heavy steam generators and other machines to move. It was estimated that the move alone would cost $100,000 in 1980 dollars, and that estimate was considered low.

The Kassams saw many of these problems and did not like what they saw. My father, given his optimistic manner, thought that the problems could be overcome. He thought that, after they rode out the storm, things would continue to get better. In fact, looking at his life, it certainly had improved since his time in Canada to that point, and one can understand why he was so optimistic. He just did not anticipate, unfortunately, the severity of the coming recession and how badly it would affect his business. In his mind, these were just business problems that some brainstorming and teamwork could solve.

The Kassams did not discuss their concerns with my father. They did not want him to know how worried they were. Just the opposite: they wanted him to buy them out. So they schemed to find a way to force him to do so. They thought that, if they went to him directly and asked him to buy them out, he would refuse because he wanted the partnership to continue. Soon they came up with a plan that forced his hand.

The Kassams knew that their use of the TFL facilities and their expenses were a sore point for my father. He had mentioned, he thought nicely to them, that it was unfair for them to be expending TFL financial resources on their personal businesses. In early 1980, the Kassams started to use the TFL facilities more often, with no holds barred. Mehbob and his father sat in the TFL offices and used the phones for long-distance calls, used the secretarial services, and ate on the company expense account. They even travelled at TFL's expense. My father asked them to stop, but they would not. He wanted to get even, but there was little opportunity for that. He did little personal travelling and did not call long distance very often. He fumed for weeks. He was losing his money to these people. My father started to consider what he could do about it. It was not a matter for the police, for what they did was not illegal. He could stop it if he was prepared for bad relations at the office. That was not in his nature.

Finally, after keeping his frustrations inside for some time, my father decided to make his partners an offer under the "shotgun buy-out" clause of their partnership agreement. That is a way of resolving otherwise unresolvable disputes among shareholders of a company. One of the shareholders makes an offer of a certain amount of money. The other shareholder has the right either to sell on the terms of the offer or to buy the offerer's shares on the same terms. It is normally a good way to resolve disputes or to dissolve partnerships, but it can work to one partner's advantage when that partner has some knowledge or expertise necessary for the operation of the business that would harm the business if it were missing.

My father didn't really want to buy out his partners or be bought out, but he realized that the partnership was finished. He could not work with them again. He confided in us. Helen and her fiancé, Victor, had been lawyers by then for almost three years. I was still an articling student, about to be called to the bar in July 1980. My business knowledge was little, and what I knew I had learned from my father. Law school does not teach a student much about the business of being a lawyer, let alone about the business world. We told our father that he should not make the offer. We thought that, if he offered an amount for the business and they accepted it, then he would be in a worse position because he would have to deal with all the company's problems himself. If he offered too little, then he would be bought out for less than what he should get. Our father listened to us and argued with us. He was 55 years old and should have been able to start winding down his business life to take things a little easier, but he mustered up his strength to overrule us all. He could run the business alone. He was a capable businessman, and things in his business would turn for the better. But he could no longer work with those people. He would make an offer, not too high, but if he got the business so be it. He didn't want to be out on the streets looking for another business again so soon, he had done enough of that in his life, and he thought that he had not yet saved enough to retire.

My father decided to offer $120,000 for the Kassam half of the business, double what he had paid for his half just three years before. He had become attached to the business, he enjoyed his position there, and his optimism caused him to miss seeing some of the upcoming problems. On a purely financial basis, it was a reasonable price. It was hard to argue that half of the business was not worth at least that, based on past performance. And in fairness to him, it was hard for anyone to predict the severity of the financial problems that would hit North America with a vengeance less than a year later in 1981.

The Kassams got the offer and decided to sell their half of the business. Until the last day, even at the closing of my father's purchase of their shares, they complained bitterly about the low price for their shares. I hated them at that time for what they had done. I believed that they had outsmarted us, and it hurt. To their complaints, my standard response was a cold one, that they could have bought my father's shares for the same price, so why bother with the crocodile tears? It didn't stop them. My father had to come up with financing to pay them out, so he took out a mortgage on his and Jenny's Vancouver home.

So, with a quick closing in the spring of 1980, he was the sole owner of TFL. My father hadn't really had time to think about the business and its problems. At first, he was feeling good about his purchase. Nothing seemed to have changed much, except that he was no longer bothered by the Kassams trying to take advantage of him. The business had experienced employees in most positions, so it kept humming along. My father was the only boss now, and he had the final say. He felt good.

Within several months, however, some big problems started to emerge. The Kassams' timing could not have been better. Interest rates continued to climb, with the prime borrowing rate reaching a new level every week. It eventually topped out at over 22 percent per year. Some TFL customers took longer to pay, forcing the company to pay the interest on inventory and receivables, and some customers did not pay at all. Bad debts climbed. TFL was also a highly leveraged business, with a lot of borrowing and little shareholder equity. The company was in debt, lots of debt, to cover the inventory of raw leather, finished jackets, payroll, receivables, machinery, and furniture. Things had been fine while interest rates were reasonable, and money had always come in sufficient time to pay the bills. But things started to get much tighter. Because of changing economic conditions, TFL's bank reviewed the outstanding loans, and though TFL had always paid every penny on time the bank now asked for a personal guarantee from our father. Helen, Victor, and I advised him not to give it. He countered that, if he did not give his personal guarantee, then the bank would not lend him anymore, and he would be unable to operate the business. He had no alternative. Besides, he fully intended to stand behind the company now that it was his responsibility alone to the bank and to everyone else. He signed the personal guarantee.

What we know now that we didn't know at the time was that there were alternatives. But as young lawyers then we were inexperienced, and our father relied on us. He didn't hire outside consultants because he had a son and a daughter and a future son-in-law as lawyers. What could some stranger advise him that his own highly educated family members could not? I blamed myself, in some ways, for this and for the rest of the failure of the business that followed soon after. I had asked my father not to buy it from the Kassams, but he had anyway. He had wanted a business so that he could support his family for several more years and then give the business to us. He had helped to educate us so that we could help him and then take over from him. He was trying to build a legacy business that he could give to us.

His factory was in Gastown, and my law office in 1980–81 was also in Gastown, only a few blocks away. After my father bought out the Kassams, I would go to TFL at lunchtime and go over things with him: the books, decisions to be made, trying to get to know the business, and so on. But I spent only an hour at most once or twice a week. I was busy with my law practice or at least busy trying to establish one. It was partly laziness but mostly that I wanted to spend time establishing my own legal career, not his business. If I had worked as hard in those days as I did later in life, or as efficiently, then maybe I could have done both. But it was impossible for me, a 25-year-old lawyer recently called to the bar, to learn the business sufficiently, in the short time that I dedicated to it, to be helpful in a meaningful way. I thought that I was smart, but I was on the wrong track. I learned quickly about law practice and management but little about real-world business. And it was painful for me to see my father floundering with some of the hard problems inherent in the business that he now owned.

Things carried on for almost a year. Our mother, bless her, knew nothing about business from her upbringing and her way of life; she simply had never had to think about it and had no interest in it. She trusted her husband completely; he was strong and capable. He was the one who had given her whatever self-confidence she had. He had always overcome adversity before. He would ride out this storm.

I was not prepared to spend sufficient time away from my law office to be a real help. Even if I had, I don't know whether there was anything that could have been done. It was Victor (Helen and Victor married in 1981) who came up with more ideas than anyone. He understood business more than the rest of us since he had been a commercial lawyer for three years. He had always been entrepreneurial, and 10 years later he quit the practice of law to go into business full time. Even Victor, though, could not help with the difficulties becoming all too apparent. It turned out that certain coloured leather inventory went out of fashion and became useless on the roll. It had to be sold well below cost. Bad debts from insolvent customers kept mounting. The move of the factory was impending, and nothing had been done to arrange it. It was a huge job to find the right location and coordinate a move. Bank interest charges went higher and higher. My father was beginning to feel completely overwhelmed by the problems and asked us to help him sell the business quickly. Victor came up with one buyer who offered little, wanted personal guarantees for all sorts of things that could not be guaranteed, but was prepared to take the business from my father. Desperate, Rubin signed the deal. When the conditions in the agreement could not be fulfilled, even though he had guaranteed that they would be, the deal collapsed, and the buyer sued my father personally.

There was little left to do. My father hated going to work now, and he hated facing the problems. We were afraid that he might have a nervous breakdown or, worse, a heart attack. One day in March 1981 Victor and I walked to the bank to inquire about its level of comfort with TFL's outstanding loan. We wanted to reinforce its concern and make it consider calling in the loan and putting in a receiver. That way my father would be relieved of having to make hard decisions day after day. The business assets would be sold, and what was left, if anything, after creditors had been paid would go to my father. Contrary to what we had hoped, the banker was delighted with him as a customer. He was ideal, always paid on time, kept the bank informed, and sent it financial statements regularly, and it could not have been happier. We hinted at what we wanted until we were blue in the face. Finally, we just told the manager straight out. Call in a receiver, sell the assets, and get your money out. If there was anything left, and we were pretty sure that there wouldn't be after payment of receiver fees and distress sale prices, the remainder would go to my father.

What followed was not a good time for him. As we suspected, after the receiver sold the assets of TFL and paid itself for doing so, there was a deficiency of over $80,000. The bank sued my father on his personal guarantee. He thought that he had nothing; most of what he had personally was in the business. He had worked hard all his life. What he had built up over the many years would now be lost (in fact, years earlier he had created some assets for himself that would serve him well, but at that time we had no idea that they would be valuable). His house had a large mortgage (the money that he had borrowed to pay the Kassams) and he had no income with which to pay it. While the receiver was selling off inventory and machinery, being at the factory was very hard on my father. He had few hobbies to take his mind off his problems. He was too downhearted even to garden. My mother was not used to having him around the house, and she had her own routine that included lots of private time for herself. She tried to be helpful, but she also didn't know how to deal with him.

Getting little from my father, the bank sued my mother for the house, claiming that the transfer of the house to her was a fraudulent conveyance made solely for my father to avoid creditors. This was not at all the case. The transfer of title from joint names to Jenny's name alone had taken place right after the house had been mortgaged to reflect the fact that my father had taken out his portion of the equity in order to buy the business. What was left was rightfully my mother's interest and should not have been affected by my father's mortgage of his half of the house. We hired a lawyer, a good friend of mine, who did a good job, but the case dragged on for months, causing my parents more worry that they would lose their home. I paid the legal bills, and finally there was a settlement with the bank for a smaller amount compared with what it could have been. The bank saw that its case was weak, but it was easier for my parents to settle than to have the claim hanging over their heads.

My father was also sued for breach of contract by a buyer with whom he had signed a purchase agreement for the business, giving representations and warranties about the business that had been true but changed daily as the business deteriorated and prevented the buyer from completing the purchase. The buyer sued for a huge amount in contract breach and lost profit.

It was then that I wished that my father had been receiving war reparations from the German government. Most European Jews who had lost their families and possessions in the Holocaust had applied for and received a monthly income, which would last for the remainder of their lives, as compensation. It was not a huge income, but it amounted to several hundred dollars a month. Most survivors of the Holocaust had applied for it. My father had always refused to apply for war reparations, saying that, if he took their money, then it would be like forgiving the Nazis for their sins. With him, forgiveness could not be bought. He never took a cent from the Germans, never bought a German-made product, never forgave them, and never forgot the horror. It was now too late to make a claim, for the Germans had allowed claims to be made for up to 10 years or so after the offer was first made. The claims had to be made by 1965 or so, although the German government did offer additional compensation plans in subsequent years. My wife's family received these reparations, as did Chasia. Rubin and Harry never wanted to. My father, even in his toughest financial times, never expressed regret over it. He was proud of not taking what he called Nazi blood money.

Helen, Max, and I were starting to worry about our parents' ability to sustain themselves. But we didn't have to worry. One wonderful thing about our father was that he always bounced back from adversity, eventually getting on with his life, making things better than before. He was able to do it again.

At heart, my father was such a positive thinker and optimistic man. But twice in his life that I knew about, he became depressed, both times when he was not working. When he was busy, he was happy. He had the most incredible urge to be useful. He was so practical. Yes, after TFL's bankruptcy, he was depressed for a while, but my father slowly worked his way out of it. And things weren't as bad financially as he had feared. He had always encouraged my mother to save money in her own name, and she had. She also had a small inheritance from her mother that had been converted to cash several years before. Although the cash total of her savings was less than the amount of their mortgage, they had a bit of luck from the source of their problems. When my father bought out his partners in 1980, he had locked in the interest rate on the mortgage for five years at a reasonable rate. More than a year later, because of much higher interest rates, my mother's money in the bank was getting more interest income than the mortgage interest payments. From the interest on the savings, they were able to pay the mortgage and some of their living expenses. High interest on savings would not last forever, but the capital was sustaining them for the time being. My father also had an ace in the hole. He still held portions of four properties in Winnipeg that he had bought or earned as commission so many years before. He was hopeful that these properties would be converted to cash in time to help pay bills in his retirement. We children were less optimistic.

The personal shame at the thought of bankruptcy of TFL had greatly upset both my parents before the decision had been made to approach the bank and at the time of the sale of TFL assets. They were both old-school, thinking that bankruptcy, even if it is not personal but just of the business, would cause their best friends to shun them. Now that the deed was done, they found that on the contrary there was no need for personal shame if their business failed. Suddenly, friends and acquaintances acknowledged that they, too, had been involved in bankruptcies, in some cases business and in others personal. No one shunned them. No one thought less of them. In fact, my father now had more time to cultivate friendships, which he had done very little of his working life until then. He also became involved in charity work for Jewish organizations, which he had also done little of while working long hours as a businessman. Charity work would become a big part of his life.

My father was still looking for a business but not with the same intensity that he had before. It took him time to overcome the feeling of being a failure. He had a business, and he had failed at it. He still felt the need to work and spent most of his time looking for something suitable.

About a year after the bankruptcy, my father decided to go back to being a real estate salesman. If he could do it in Winnipeg, then why couldn't he do it in Vancouver? As he prepared for the exams, though, he found that he no longer could study for and pass a difficult exam based on memorizing law, policy, rules, and tables. There were financial and actuarial tables to remember and work with, statistics, regulations, and codes of ethics. He knew all the aspects of being a real estate agent instinctively, but he was almost 60. His memory wasn't as good as it had been, and he hadn't studied for an exam of any kind in about 40 years. He couldn't write down on an exam paper under pressure the answers that the Real Estate Board was looking for. He failed the exam on the first try, as many do, but his self-esteem took another downswing. He went back to looking for a small business.

About three years after TFL's bankruptcy, when the worst was over, and the personal lawsuits had been settled or were dormant, my father bought a dry-cleaning business. It was not an easy living or a lucrative one. In buying this type of business, he had come to the realization that his choices were limited.

Being a self-starter and always very motivated, he was prepared to do what had to be done to make the best of his situation. My mother's savings were used to buy the business assets, consisting of machinery and leasehold improvements. The dry cleaner was located in a strip mall on 49th Avenue and Oak Street in Vancouver, close to the Jewish landmarks of the city. My father ran the business himself, taking in the laundry and putting it through the machines. He was busy and starting to feel better about himself. After a short while, he started talking and joking with his customers. Many were people who knew him or knew someone else in the Pinsky family. His customers started to become regulars and enjoyed meeting him. My father could do this job. True, it was not very complicated, but he had lost a lot of confidence over the previous several years. Now he started to enjoy what he was doing; he had a place to go in the morning and customers who enjoyed doing business with him. He made just enough money to make it worthwhile working. He was feeling better. So much better, we all thought, that he was even starting to slim down after being quite overweight.

Seemingly overnight, though, in the mid-1980s, my father started to slim down considerably. He also started to have problems with his eyes. He could not move them easily, and they even started to bulge. He went to his family doctor, who praised him for his loss of weight. When the rest of the family expressed concern about his rapid weight loss and especially about his eyes, the doctor decided that the changes had been caused by stress in our father's life. As anyone who has read this account so far knows, there had been a lot of stress at many times of his life, but right then was not one of those times. But who were we, his children and lawyers all, to question the medical opinion of his doctor? Yet our father lost more weight, and his eyes looked worse and worse.

It was finally a customer at the dry-cleaning establishment, not even a doctor but a doctor's wife, who diagnosed my father on sight with hyperactive thyroid condition. She saw his eyes bulging out of their sockets and said immediately that he had better see a specialist about his illness. My father had never heard of this condition, but as soon as he was tested by the specialist it was a clear case of hyperactive thyroid with classic symptoms. Unfortunately, his condition was advanced. Because it had not been caught in time, over the next two years he had to undergo three operations on his eyes. As soon as he started on the thyroid drugs, he returned to his normal overweight state. My father simply ate too much to stay slim. And because he had to have eye surgery, which would require considerable time to heal, he was forced to sell the dry-cleaning business that he had now operated for over two years. It was also the end of his income from work and his business career.

In 1986, my parents sold their house on 64th Avenue to move to a condominium on Heather Street and West 27th Avenue in Vancouver. It was a great move for them. They got enough money for the house on 64th Avenue so that they could buy the condo without a mortgage. This was a relief from a monthly payment burden. As well, the condo was smaller than their house and therefore more manageable. Two people did not need so many bedrooms, there was no yard to tend, and the location was terrific. They were happy there from the day they moved in.

In 1987, my father received more bad news that turned, ironically and eventually, into good news. He was still a partner with three others—including Harry, a lawyer, and another businessman—in a piece of property on the edge of the developed area of Winnipeg. My father had been inactive for several reasons in the management of the Winnipeg properties in which he had an interest. First, they were not worth much. Second, he could not do the management from Vancouver. Third, he had his brother in Winnipeg who, he thought, would look after his interests. The other partners, who all lived in Winnipeg, had requisitioned money in 1987 from each partner to pay the expenses, such as annual taxes, because for several years the tenant farmer either had not paid rent or there had been no tenant. In prior years when there was a cash call on the partners and my father had the money, he would grudgingly pay. Grudgingly because it was almost unbelievable to him that after over 25 years, with no mortgage on the property, it could not pay for itself. However, that was the reality in Winnipeg, far different from the buoyant real estate market in Vancouver. For this cash call in 1987, however, my father simply could not pay his share. He told his partners that he could not pay it. The amount was not a lot, under $2,000. But it's a lot if you don't have the money. If our father had talked to us, we would have helped, but he didn't. He never asked us for financial help.

In Winnipeg, his partners were becoming impatient. The lawyer partner wasn't prepared to support the property without my father's share of the expenses paid. The lawyer was not only a shareholder in the company that owned the land but also a company director and its lawyer. He told Harry that a partner who doesn't pay his share of cash calls defaults on his shares in the company that owns the property. The remaining partners sent notice to my father that, if he did not pay within a stipulated time, his shares in the company would be forfeited. He could do nothing about the payment at that time. His shares were forfeited to the three other partners, and they paid his assessment.

Enter the lawyers. We found out about this almost by chance. Our father showed Helen the letter that purported to rob him of his interest in the property. We held a meeting, the four lawyers in the family (Victor, Helen, me, and Max, who had become a lawyer in 1984), and reviewed the law. Under clear law, shares that have been fully paid and issued (which our father's had been decades before) could not be seized except under a court order. We decided to sue on his behalf the land-holding company and its three shareholders for doing what in our view was clearly not permitted under the law or the terms of the agreement that governed the relationship of the shareholders. We sued them all, including Harry. We also claimed against the lawyer a breach of his responsibilities and duties as a lawyer, company director, and manager of the property.

The lawsuit had to be filed in Manitoba because that's where the property was. We therefore had to hire lawyers in Manitoba to file the case. However, several months after we had instructed the lawyers in Winnipeg, we were not at all satisfied with the job that they were doing. The case that they wanted to advance in the statement of claim was not strongly or fully stated in our opinion. We wanted the claim to be so clear that the case would be won before the matter got to the next step in the proceedings. The four of us sat for hours one night and formulated a tough, tight, winning claim that we thought was sure to scare the heck out of all the defendants. The claim was all true and legal and drafted in such a way as to show what the defendants had done improperly. It was the first time that I can truly say we were of great help to our father. We sent off the revised statement of claim and told the lawyers to file it in court. They did so and served it on each defendant. It scared them and how!

Shortly after the defendants received the claims, I went to Winnipeg on business. I called my uncle Harry, as I always did when I visited there. I told him that we were sorry to have to sue him as well as the others, but legally we had no choice because he was in the same legal position as they were since he had been involved in the action to take my father's interest in the land. Harry told me that he wanted to see me immediately, and I was glad to do so. When we got together, he told me that he had been assured by the lawyer/partner that foreclosing my father from his shares in the property had to be done, and Harry had gone along with it only because he thought that he had no choice. But there was some hope; the lawyer/partner asked Harry to arrange a meeting with me right away to potentially work out a settlement. We had the meeting; I was asked whether I had authority to settle the case for my father, which I did, and within a day I had a full settlement agreement and a cheque for the purchase of my father's shares in an amount that, together with what my mother had left from the sale of the dry-cleaning business, was sufficient to give my parents some measure of security. They were not wealthy by any means, but the interest on their capital could now sustain a modest life for them. My father had been right to buy land in Winnipeg after all!

Starting in 1988, my father began to busy himself almost full time with volunteer work. This was perfectly fine with my mother, who had been involved with volunteer work all her married life. She was a member for life of several Jewish women's organizations because of the time and effort that she had dedicated. In Vancouver, one of the charities that she volunteered for was the Kosher Food Bank. She started to take her husband along, and they packed food into hampers and passed it out to the waiting crowds. This was a once-a-week activity.

One day the Food Bank's food buyer was sick. The buyer was the person allotted a certain amount of money and expected to buy whatever kosher food she could, the more the better. The buyer had her usual places to get food. The head of the Food Bank asked my father if he could help that day and do the buying. Boy, did they hit the jackpot! He was an incredible bargain hunter. My father went out with the money allotted by the Food Bank and spent all day and some of the next day getting bargains of all sorts, canned food and bread, packaged food and flour, juice, and every other type of non-perishable that a person could find. He bargained, compared, drove from store to store, asked to speak to managers, bargained some more. He bought almost twice as much food as had the regular buyer with the same amount of money. He was an instant hit, and from then on for several years he was one of the volunteer buyers of the Food Bank. He had a lot of fun doing it too.

The other organization that my father became very involved in was the Vancouver Holocaust Education Centre (VHEC). VHEC was expanding in the Jewish Community Centre and was prepared to house a museum and memorial to the Holocaust so that people who were not familiar with it could learn about the atrocities and never allow something like that to happen again. My father was appointed to the board of directors of VHEC and helped to create it, devoting time and effort to fundraising for it but even more importantly getting Holocaust survivors to donate their memorabilia to the museum. He was quite successful in both endeavours. In 1994, when the VHEC became a reality, he could consider it to be partly his success.

His other time started to fill too. My father started to get together with men his age to have coffee or play poker once or twice a week. He went for long walks with my mother and was one of the prime movers in a once-a-month Yiddish speakers' group. My parents started to see their friends more often, and my father continued his theological debates with whoever would accept his challenge. When Max and his wife, Leona, were most involved in a new, "hip" style of synagogue, Or Shalom, which called itself traditional egalitarian but in many ways was particularly spiritual, with singing and chanting as major parts of the service, my father became a regular attendee. In short order, he became the "elder statesman" to be consulted on matters of religion. His knowledge of the Torah and other Jewish laws, customs, and rules never left him. He remembered his pre-1940 Jewish studies as if he had just completed them. He spoke Hebrew well, though his language was somewhat archaic and biblical, and he was willing to go to Or Shalom and be a resource. My father did not do it for the honour, but it did make him feel appreciated. He knew Judaism and believed that he should pass along his knowledge to the next generation. He passed along his religious knowledge despite not believing in God. He always said, if asked, that God was dead, but the casual observer might have thought that he was religious. The Jewish way of life was how my father had been brought up, and he was willing to pass along to the next generation what he knew about Jewish religion, history, and culture.

In late 1983, he became a grandfather, with more grandchildren coming along regularly until there were nine. He was a wonderful grandfather, and his grandchildren loved going to his house, where they would play games with him, watch nature shows, and get their favourite foods. In the summer, my father would take them down to Douglas Park, where there was lots of action. He was always willing to drive his grandchildren to where they needed to go or to pick them up from school if mom and dad were unable to do so. We didn't know that starting in the mid-1980s and increasingly our father did most and then eventually everything needed for his grandchildren when he and our mother were with them. Her dementia developed quickly and prevented her to a greater and greater degree from being involved with them.

His life thus filled with things that my father never would have considered doing while he was working, and he thus became contented. Even financially, things got better for him. In 1991, Victor, Helen's husband, quit law to become a businessman. He headed a public company that initially was trading on the Alberta Stock Exchange and invested in some oil and gas pipelines in Oklahoma. Victor needed a director for the public company who had business experience and whom he could trust. He asked my father to be one of the directors and in return gave him stock options exercisable at the price that the shares were trading on the date of Rubin's appointment, standard for stock options. The share price did not increase for a long time, but then in late 1993 Victor's company entered a deal with a high-tech company for the development of some computer memory hardware. The market liked the idea a lot, and the company's stock price rose considerably. My father not only exercised his options and sold his shares to make an excellent profit but also offered a portion of his options to his children. He gave us the right to exercise a number of options at the set price and to keep any profit on the sale of those optioned shares. Max and I made some capital gains at a time when it was greatly appreciated. Money is always appreciated, but for both me and my father it came at a good time in our lives. I had recently bought a new house, and my mortgage payments were high. My parents had been okay financially because they had been frugal. Now they had enough of a cushion that they didn't have to worry about every penny. My father was still frugal, and like his purchasing for the Kosher Food Bank his personal money always went a long way.

CHAPTER 16

Final Years

In the late 1990s, my father's health deteriorated. His memory was not so good, his ability to concentrate was poor, and his diabetes would soon give him serious trouble.

In the summer of 1997 at age 72, my father had a serious stroke. We found out about it hours later; he had the stroke and then drove to his bank for a meeting with his bank manager. He sat with the banker and couldn't say anything; no words came out of his mouth. Maybe the bank manager called an ambulance since by then my mother wouldn't have been able to do so. We went to the hospital to see him, and the sight of him in that hospital bed brought me to tears. He was always strong, my father, at least in my eyes. In that bed, he looked frail, and he couldn't talk or move his left side. It shocked my sister-in-law, Leona, that I cried; she had never seen me cry. It shocked me too.

My father stayed in the hospital, and my mother came to live with my family during his hospital stay. It was then that we realized how much her Alzheimer's had progressed and how much my father had been covering for it. In the weeks that my mother stayed with us, she never remembered which bedroom she slept in and how to get to it. She followed us around the house and did simple things that she was asked, such as sit, eat, or go with us somewhere. She mostly sat around and pretended to read a book or magazine.

When my father came out of the hospital, he and my mother went back to their condo. He used a walker and spoke with great difficulty. His brain had been severely affected by the stroke too. My parents couldn't take care of themselves to any extent, let alone care for each other. The family arranged for caregivers to be at their home 16 hours a day, except when they slept. That later changed to 24 hours a day. We immediately applied for them to be admitted to the Louis Brier Home and Hospital, a Jewish seniors' home. That they needed to be cared for and that they needed a Jewish seniors' home were evident, and waiting times weren't so bad in those days. About five months after we applied, my parents were admitted to two adjoining rooms in January 1998 at the Louis Brier. Before they went in, they complained that they wanted to stay at home, and Shia Moser, my mother's cousin, spoke to us to push us in that direction. But Helen, Max, and I agreed that what our parents needed was full-time care, and we could not provide that care if they stayed in their home. Luckily, as soon as they moved in, they enjoyed the Louis Brier and were very happy there despite their earlier misgivings.

In July 1998, Max and Leona had their fourth child, Rina. Rina was in physical distress when she was born and underwent four major operations in her first 10 days of life. She was diagnosed with a severe case of cystic fibrosis, a disease that is always fatal. Max and Leona fought for Rina's life in every way that parents can, but after about a month the doctors told them that Rina's systems were failing and that she was about to pass away. They advised that friends and family be called to the hospital immediately to say their goodbyes.

I brought Rubin in his wheelchair to see Rina after explaining the situation to him. Everyone in the family had reluctantly accepted that the end for Rina was imminent. All except

Rubin. He didn't say goodbye to her; he spoke to her like a grandfather would to any healthy baby. I whispered to him, "Dad, say goodbye." He answered, "She's going to make it." I told him that the doctors had clearly said that she wouldn't and that we have to accept it. "No," he answered quietly, "I feel she's going to make it." A day later Rina rallied. The doctors were thankfully all proven wrong, and thanks to the unbelievable dedication of her parents, and big breakthroughs in treatment in the past decade, Rina celebrated her 25th birthday as this book went to publication.

My father improved over time. He could speak better and walked around the Louis Brier leaning on his walker with more confidence. He participated in music therapy and the Yiddish group and most other activities that didn't involve physical movement or exercise. He got into a comfortable routine; for example, he would follow the cookie tray around and take an extra cookie or two at teatime, and despite his diabetes we no longer scolded him.

In August 2001, my father was sent to UBC Hospital (UBCH) for a "tune-up." The doctors didn't know exactly what was wrong, but the Louis Brier medical staff wanted him checked. The morning of August 23, I got a call at home as I was about to leave for work. A Jewish doctor was on the line, someone I didn't know. But he knew that my father was Jewish, so he had taken on the responsibility of calling me even though my father wasn't his patient. The doctor started with "Has anyone called you yet?" No one had. "Your father's vital statistics are not good. You should come." I dropped something off at work and cancelled my appointments and went to UBCH.

My father was lying in bed there, his breath laboured. He couldn't talk. I sat with him, holding his hand, talking to him to pass the time, and I tried to reach my siblings by phone but couldn't. I told my father that I loved him, and time passed as I watched him, holding his hand and chatting about things that we did together and other things that came to my mind. After a couple of hours, he jerked a bit, then relaxed. His eyes were open, but he didn't breathe. I called the nurse, but he was gone.

At the funeral held the next day, I wheeled my mother in front of us to the graveside and back, but it was clear that she didn't understand what was going on. She was mentally and emotionally spared the loss of her husband.

My father had lived a full life, and before he went to the Louis Brier we tried to protect his health, which we now know can't be done for someone else. Because he had diabetes and was overweight, when we wanted to take away some sweet or pastry from him since it was bad for his heart or his diabetes, or when we admonished him for being too fat, he said with a grin that he should stay fat for another 20 years, and he would be happy. *Halevai!* ("I wish it could be so!") He didn't last 20 years, but for most of his life he was happy anyway.

CHAPTER 17

My Father's Character

The story of my father imparts only a portion of his character. We loved him as a father, no one could ask for a better one, though we did not see him as much as we wanted when we were growing up. On one occasion, when as a young teen I had done something much worse than usual (I don't remember what), my mother thought that she had to threaten me with some punishment worse than she could administer. She told me that my father would punish me when he got home. Sure enough, when he came home at 8 or 8:30, she filled his ear before he had dinner with my bad or simply mischievous behaviour. He took off his belt and headed into my room, my mother telling me that what was about to happen was for my own good. He closed the door and looked stern. Any other father, coming home from a 12-hour day, hungry, and expected to please his wife, would have meted out the punishment that I probably did deserve. Instead, my father told me to cry out when I heard the whacking sound. He cracked his belt several times either on the wooden part of the bed or on something else that made a loud noise, and I cried out, trying not to laugh. After that, I didn't come out of my room for hours, pretending to sniffle with my pride hurt as much as my bottom. It got to the point where my mother chastised my father through his dinner for being too hard on me. He never let on, and neither did I.

He loved discussions about Judaism and religion in general. Perhaps because he was so familiar with them, he could debate for hours about subjects that one would expect only rabbis to think about. These discussions invariably could be extrapolated to become relevant to everyday life, as religious topics tend to do. My father was interested in a great many other things, but he never became much of an expert in any of them. He could, and did, watch nature shows on television for hours. He would tape the shows—about whales, tigers, insects, you name it—for his grandchildren, none of whom, unfortunately, inherited the same degree of fascination with nature that he had. He loved corny things, simple things, such as jugglers on *The Ed Sullivan Show* and low-grade comedy. In his good days, he was easily made happy. In the rare periods when he was depressed, sometimes nothing could make him happy.

In the late 1980s and when he wasn't at Or Shalom synagogue, my father started going with my mother to her synagogue on Saturdays. At first, it was to be a good husband. Later he would go whether my mother did or not. He would, with her cousin Izzie Moser, start checking out different synagogues on Saturday mornings. He would also accompany my mother to Friday-night services if time permitted after the family dinner.

Our parents instilled a sense of family in us that is rare today. While they were alive, we all lived in Vancouver within a relatively short drive from our parents' home. During our parents' lives and beyond until COVID-19, we siblings had a Shabbat dinner for the whole family every Friday, with not only our parents and each of our nuclear families but also others in the extended family and even friends. The average Friday dinner from the 1980s to about 2010 was 16 to 18 people, including kids. The big dinners were more than 30 people. My mother cooked for all at her home every Friday for many years until, in the early 1980s, before any of us had children, it became too much for her. Helen and I started taking turns for a Friday each month, and Max and Leona started taking a monthly turn when they got married. Until our father's stroke, Shabbat dinner was at each one's house once every four weeks. To our knowledge, there are few other families who made that much effort to get together every week.

For everything that we learned about life from our father, little of it was what he told us. He was a man of few words, especially when it came to frank and open talks with us. It was what he did, how he did it, what he enthused about or frowned upon that showed us how to grow up to be a *mentsch* (a "good person"). Our father was the most reliable person whom you could ever meet, always keeping his word on anything that he said. He was ever helpful, coming over cheerfully to pack us up if we were moving or going on a trip, coming to babysit, drive us to the airport, or shovel our snow.

After he passed away and for the next few years, I would be at some event, say a film at the Jewish Film Festival, and someone whom I didn't really know but looked vaguely familiar (I have a terrible memory for faces) would say to me something like "You're Rubin's son. I miss him. A few years ago he helped me translate my mother's letters from Yiddish to English, and it meant so much to me!" Or someone from Or Shalom might say "Rubin was so helpful to us. I remember that he would come to the synagogue soon after Yom Kippur and set up the Sukkah for our congregation." I was astounded at how many people would have a nice story and remembrance of my father helping in some way, things that he had never told me or anyone else in the family. He was quietly and regularly doing good in the world, not seeking special thanks or recognition. What seemed like an ordinary life was more than that in so many ways. I'll always think of him as my ordinary, extraordinary father.

PART II

The Roots Trip I Never Thought I Would Take

In May and June 2012, my wife, Daniella; my brother, Max; his son, Simon; our cousin Lawrence, the son of Harry Pinsky, and his wife, Jennifer; and I, the six of us, met in Warsaw to start our journey to Belarus to go to the town where Rubin Pinsky grew up: Djatlovo or Gzetl, its Yiddish name. I was so excited and nervous about it that I needed a mechanism to focus my thoughts and calm me; that mechanism was writing a blog, which I had not done before and haven't done since. Not only did it calm me, but also it lifted from my mind the burden of having to concentrate on remembering everything—I wrote down what I thought was important, and reading it in the future would jog my memory. That thinking turned out to work well.

This blog appeared (and still does) starting May 29, 2012, at rootstrip.wordpress.com. In the online blog, the last blog post appears at the top, and all blogs appear in reverse order, so this compilation is easier to follow. The blog still gets some traffic every year, more than 10 years after the last blog post, in 2012, but while I was posting them they were getting 300–400 hits a day. That is nothing compared with today's "influencer" numbers, I admit, but at the time it showed real interest by my friends and family members. I certainly enjoyed the positive feedback left by some of the readers. I hope that these blog posts give the reader a sense of what we travellers were feeling.

MAY 29, 2012

A Trip a Long Time in the Making

There are two lasting bequests we can give our children:
One is roots, the other is wings.
—Hodding Carter II, journalist, editor, and author

I admit that I do this, *all* of this, with trepidation. My dad never wanted to . . . so why should I? He said that he would never go back, that he wanted to move on with his life, and, boy, did he ever. He was never a bitter person; he was so positive despite everything that had happened.

So now it is up to me, my brother, and our cousin, together with two spouses and one son, to see the old country where my dad, Rubin, and his brother, Harry, were born and raised, where their parents and sister were murdered, where Harry was conscripted into the Russian army, where Rubin and his other sister, Chasia, escaped into the forests of Poland and lived under the trees for almost three years. Where Rubin almost died many times, where he ended up a teenager with a gun, fighting for his life. We are going to Djatlovo, Belarus, or as Rubin and Harry knew it, Gzetl, Poland. It is the same place.

The story of how we are on the verge of leaving on a roots trip started almost 17 years ago. As a gift for his 72nd birthday in 1996, and because I thought that his life story had to be told, I wrote the story of my father's life in a short book titled *Ordinary, Extraordinary: My Father's Life*. I gave it to my father, but I don't know that he ever read it. By then, he'd had a severe stroke, and he wasn't up to reading anymore. But he was pleased with the attention, he was happy, and so was everyone in the family. I didn't publish the book, but I sent it to relatives whom I thought would be interested. (I am going to post the book on the internet and post the link in this blog in the not-too-distant future.) It is a fascinating story, in my view at least, and about half the book is on his life in the town in which he was raised, Gzetl, Poland, and his experiences in the Holocaust.

Among those to whom I sent the book was my cousin once removed, Melvin Fenson (of blessed memory), in Jerusalem. Melvin read the book and decided to submit it to the national Holocaust museum in Jerusalem, Yad Vashem. It sat there for over 10 years, and I didn't think anything more of it, when around 2007 I got a letter from someone who identified herself as a Catholic high school teacher in a town in Belarus called Djatlovo. I had never heard of the town, but it turned out to be my dad's town, Gzetl, transformed by the Russian soldiers who had populated it after the war and by the change of borders. The teacher, Zhanna, had found my book at Yad Vashem while she was doing research on the history of her town, and she asked my permission to translate the book into Russian. She wanted to use it for the little history wing of the high school!

Of course, I said yes. I tried to contact Zhanna on more than one occasion, I even phoned her at home, but she speaks no English, and I speak no Russian (that was before the computer translation programs were even slightly accurate). So we didn't have an easy time communicating. I even had a hard time knowing what was going on, not sure how to figure it out. But then things took a dramatic turn. My brother, Max, and his daughter went to Djatlovo in February 2009, just like that! That trip changed *everything*.

There is much more to this story—stay tuned.

*

MAY 31, 2012

Max Led the Way

In February 2009, my brother, Max, and his daughter, Rachael, decided to find this schoolteacher, Zhanna, who had left her native Belarus and travelled to Jerusalem to find out about the history of her small town. Djatlovo is now about 10,000 people. The vast majority are the descendants of the Russian soldiers who fought against the Nazis and eventually succeeded in pushing them out of Russia, then out of Poland, and then back into Germany. As a sign of gratitude for their efforts, Russia gave these brave soldiers homes to live in. There was only one catch: the homes that the Russians so generously gave to their soldiers were not the Russians' homes to give. The homes belonged to real people. True, many of those homeowners were dead, and many of them didn't have any surviving relatives, but some of the homeowners did survive, and if they didn't survive someone else in the family might have survived. A technicality, as far as the Russians were concerned. The homes went to those whom they decided needed them.

So now, in 2009, the homes of the over 3,500 Jews who had lived in Djatlovo, Belarus (formerly Gzetl, Poland), were no longer Jewish homes. There was very little if anything left of the Jewish presence there from prior to the Second World War. People there knew either little or nothing about the hundreds of years of Jewish presence. But some brave souls, Zhanna among them, were interested in the history of the town and prepared to do something about it.

When Max and Rachael arrived in February 2009, it was like they went back to Winnipeg. The country was flat and cold, with snow on the ground. But the reception that they got was so, so warm. Zhanna and the other high school teachers had arranged a special assembly of all high school teachers and students who spoke English, and they put on a presentation for Max and Rachael that lasted almost four hours. Students spoke about the country, the province, and the town; they explained the culture, the people, the geography, and the industry; and they proudly told Max and Rachael all about themselves. It is hard to believe, but Max took lots of video, and we have seen it. It is quite amazing. And then those students and teachers started asking questions about Max and Rachael and the family, and Canada, and our life here, and their views on all kinds of things. They were genuinely interested and excited to have Max and Rachael there. It was quite an honour for them, and they came away very moved.

So, when Max told me that now his son, Simon, wants to go to Djatlovo, how could I not go with him? And, if we were going, how could we not tell our cousin Lawrence? And Daniella and Lawrence's wife, Jennifer, are coming to protect their husbands from their emotions. So we are a merry band of six.

We are arriving there in a few days.

*

JUNE 2, 2012

My Book: It's not Fair!

An ounce of performance is worth a pound of promises.
—Mae West, actor, singer, comedian, screenwriter, and playwright

OK, so I admit that technically it is not a book; it is a "manuscript." A "book" is a manuscript that has been published, and this one has not been. To be published, it needs to be professionally edited, reviewed (and likely rejected) by a publisher, and negotiated regarding costs and royalties, and so on.* I was not interested in going through all that, and I certainly don't care about the money; I just wanted to honour my father. I wanted my family members and friends to know that, though my father seemed like such an ordinary man, he both was and wasn't, at the same time. I suppose that this is true of most people. So I never tried to get it published; I just sent it to family members, and if someone expressed a particular interest I emailed it to them or lent it to them. Their reviews, admittedly biased, all from people who care about us, were pretty good. By the way, my father, of blessed memory, passed away in 2001.

But now things are changed. It is not fair to readers of this blog (anybody out there?) for me to keep talking about this book that resulted in a seminal and emotional trip for me and some of my family members to keep hearing about the book but not get a chance to read it if they choose to do so. So I asked my son Eitan to put it up for me on an internet site, and he did it right away. I was going to wait until after my trip so that I could check places, names, do one last read through. I'm a lawyer, after all!** But in fairness to those who need to know a bit more in order to keep them interested in this blog, I have posted the book, *Ordinary, Extraordinary: My Father's Life*, at the following website: eitanpinsky.com/wp-content/uploads/2012/06/Ordinary-Extraordinary-My-Fathers-Life.pdf.***

It is 70 pages long, or just over 47,000 words, posted in PDF format. To give you perspective, the average book is 80,000 words. So it can be called a "manuscriptella" (I made that up as related to "novella") because it is like a manuscript, only shorter. To understand my trip and why I need to do this, if you read until my father arrives in Canada and no more, then you will have it.

The other reason that I am providing access to the book now is that I probably won't write another post for five or six days. I won't arrive in Warsaw until Wednesday, and we don't get to Belarus until Thursday. I don't want to lose your interest for lack of material.

I hope that you enjoy it.

* *This 2023 book that you are reading is self-published.*

** *I resigned from the legal profession on December 31, 2021.*

*** *The site is no longer in existence.*

*

JUNE 9, 2012

It's an Adventure, not a Vacation

It is 4:20 a.m., June 9, 2012, and the partygoers just under our hotel window have reduced their noise level from screaming at the tops of their lungs to just loud talking, so I can still hear their voices through our closed windows. I have slept less than two hours tonight, and less than four hours last night, and every nerve in my body is racing like a Ferrari. This is just the latest in a series of events that have reminded me, over and over again, that this is an adventure and not a holiday: not everything is going to go as smoothly as I hoped. That is not to say that I am not in good spirits, because I truly am, or that this has not been an incredible journey for me, because in two short days in Belarus it has already been one of the most emotionally challenging yet satisfying trips of my life. Much, much more on that very soon in future blogs. Now I want to set the stage for what has occurred.

Daniella and I met in Toronto, on cue, and caught our flight to London. The flight left Toronto about 45 minutes late, and we knew that the delay could spell trouble, because our connection at Heathrow was just 70 minutes. I don't know why anyone would sell an airline ticket when a connection at Heathrow is less than two and a half hours, even if the first plane lands on time. It just takes a lot of time at Heathrow with security and finding gates and so on. I decided early on not to get upset, so I didn't. Even when we were told that the next flight to Warsaw was seven hours later, so that we would miss our entire day there and arrive in the evening instead of the morning, we decided to read our books and just relax, which we did.

However, when we finally did arrive at Warsaw, my suitcase, which had been tagged "priority" because I have Air Canada elite status, did not arrive. Daniella's did. Clerks at the Lost and Found were sympathetic, but, no, they had no idea where it was, and, no, they couldn't send it to anywhere but a major airport when it did arrive. It would probably arrive the next afternoon. Could we stay in Warsaw another day? The trouble was that we had planned on spending a day in Warsaw (which we had spent at Heathrow), and our train would leave Warsaw at 7:30 the next morning. We had already lost any spare time that we had. To make a long story short, we left without my bag early the next morning. We took two trains, crossed over the border into Belarus, and then were picked up by a private driver. We were seven hours of travel away from Warsaw when we got the call that the bag had been found. Our "fixer," Yuri, tried to make all kinds of plans to get the bag to me, but in the end all of them meant a day's journey in our otherwise very tight schedule just to get it. I decided to forgo my suitcase until I got back to Warsaw at the end of my trip. I bought some basics—socks, underwear, a shirt, a toothbrush—but you will understand when you see my pictures on a future blog (a hope, not a promise, because nothing is easy in Belarus) and I am wearing the same shirt in every picture.

A major reason that I decided to forgo my suitcase is that very little goes smoothly or quickly in Belarus. Take yesterday's breakfast. The hotel manager told our guide/translator/arranger Yuri, whom I will call our fixer for short, that we would have breakfast at 9 a.m. At that time, she told us that she hadn't arranged anything, and she would take us to a friend's restaurant (this is a small town, and there are no breakfast restaurants). We waited 20 minutes; then she changed her mind and told us that she would serve us at a table outside. That would be good since it was a nice day. Then half an hour later, with no food yet served, we found out that we could get our food in the bar in the basement, which still smelled like beer from the night before. The food was fine, but you are probably beginning to get the drift.

Speaking of the hotel (the only hotel in Djatlovo), Yuri told us many times that for a small town (9,000 inhabitants) it was a hotel of very good quality and very cheap. When we got our room, it did look decent, but there was a not-so-faint smell of sewage in the bathroom. It was cheap, yes, but more than twice what our fixer said it would cost. Yes, our room was clean (we were staying there for four nights) and roomy, but our bed squealed like a banshee if we made the slightest move in it, the sewage smell went away until we ran the water, which was pretty often when we were in the room, and as I started this blog Djatlovo party headquarters seemed to be right under our window.

One other quick point: this was clearly a police state. When we wanted to have a picnic on the grass in front of City Hall in town yesterday, Yuri told us that there is a national law that prohibits *more than three people* from gathering together in any public place. The law is rarely enforced, but the police could easily threaten to arrest us if we gathered together to eat our lunch if they chose to (we were eight people, six Pinskys, Yuri, and a local driver). There were police and army personnel in abundance. No one jay-walks, and no one crosses the street on red, even if there are no approaching cars. I think everyone knows that they are being watched all the time.

Yet I am so emotionally high. We have met two teachers here whom I would put into the category of saints for their work in preserving the memory of the Holocaust and for teaching tolerance of and respect for other cultures to their students, in an otherwise very homogeneous population. Much more in blogs to come soon, I promise.

A hint: I have been asked to deliver a speech tonight to the high school graduating class and the hundreds of well wishers, family members, and friends in attendance at the graduation ceremony. It is the first time *ever* that foreigners have come to this event. As I said, I am revving. I just hope that I don't run out of gas before the finish line.

PS: after writing this, I slept another two and a half hours. All is well with the world.

*

JUNE 11, 2012

The Saints of Belarus

In the Jewish religion, there is no concept of a saint, but there is a word for a person who embodies many of a saint's qualities. The word is *tsadik*, meaning a "great," "noble," or "righteous" person, and the word is closely related to the Hebrew word *tsedek*, which means "justice."

In two small towns in Belarus, we found two such *tsadiks*. Both happened to be named Zhanna, which we were told is not such a common name here. Zhanna Nagavonskaya, whom Max had met in his previous visit to Belarus, is a history teacher in the Djatlovo high school. Djatlovo is an isolated town of about 9,000 souls in west-central Belarus, not particularly significant in any way except to our family. It is the town where my father and his family were born and lived up to 1942. In 2002, Zhanna took part in the annual memorial march to the local cemeteries, where the people of Djatlovo laid flowers on graves in respect for those buried in the town. She noticed that for some reason no one ever laid flowers in what was by far the largest cemetery in town, the Jewish cemetery. She became curious.

Her curiosity led Zhanna to discover that two-thirds of the town had been Jewish until the Second World War, when most of the town's Jews were murdered by the Nazis. Those who survived emigrated to other countries. The history of the town before the war was virtually unknown. Zhanna petitioned the national authorities to let her find out and teach her high school students about those events. At first, the authorities resisted, but over time they relented and gave her permission but provided no resources. Using her own free time, Zhanna interviewed seniors in the town, and what she found out led her farther and farther afield. After some years, she went to Israel to meet former Djatlovo residents who had survived and could describe in great detail both the vibrant Jewish life in town before the war and the terrible destruction that came starting in 1941, when the Nazis occupied it.

With help from other teachers and some of her students, Zhanna has created a small room in her high school that serves as a museum of the Jewish history of Djatlovo. Today she leads symposiums for high school students from Djatlovo and other towns where she teaches Holocaust studies and Jewish history of the region, in addition to her other history subjects. She says that she believes in the importance of this project so strongly because of her faith (she is Russian Orthodox). Her faith drives her to give respect to other peoples besides her own religious compatriots, and her lessons teach a powerful anti-racism message.

The other Zhanna, Zhanna Kasperovitch (whom I will call Zhanna K), is equally dedicated. She lives in Ivusevichi, a town about 85 kilometres south of Djatlovo. Zhanna K had heard some talk of Jews being massacred around her town in the Second World War, but she saw no signs of the events. When she took a course in law in the 2000s as part of her studies (she is also a high school teacher), she learned the importance of documenting evidence, because without hard evidence stories are forgotten or misconstrued over time. Zhanna K decided to investigate and gather hard evidence of the treatment of her fellow townspeople by the Nazis. What she found shocked her, and the stories could not fully convey the horrors of what had taken place. The more she learned, the more she wanted to memorialize publicly the innocent victims. She applied for state funding to establish appropriate memorials to mark sites of atrocities, and after being rejected many times she finally persevered. This was extremely significant because the Belarus government had always refused to acknowledge the Jewish nature of the Holocaust or that the vast majority of the Nazi victims in Belarus, possibly numbering in the millions, were Jews. All prior memorials at massacre sites were dedicated to innocent citizens of Belarus and did not refer to the fact that most victims were Jews. In many massacres, the Jews alone of whole towns were taken to sites and killed, 2,000–5,000 at a time. Today Zhanna K is an expert on Holocaust education in Belarus and takes part in symposia; she continues to work tirelessly to memorialize those who perished.

The two Zhannas are doing all this work in their own time and completely selflessly. I found it such an honour to be in the presence of such righteous persons, ordinary citizens who have dedicated themselves to justice and simply to doing what they believe to be the right thing. Neither of the Zhannas understands English, but through an interpreter we could only begin to tell them how much we admire and appreciate them. Thank you, our Zhannas, for being the righteous people that you are.

*

JUNE 12, 2012

Graduation Day

On Saturday afternoon, June 9, we attended Djatlovo's high school graduation. There are three schools, and all 32 children graduated together in a ceremony and extravaganza involving most of the town.

The ceremony started at 4 p.m. in the town square. Thousands lined up around the square and heard speeches from dignitaries, were introduced to the graduates, and were entertained by singing and dancing by the graduates themselves. This outdoors portion lasted about an hour and a quarter. Unfortunately, it rained much of the time, and hard for at least 20 minutes. People opened their umbrellas and stuck it out the whole time. We didn't have umbrellas and got totally soaked.

The graduates were Grade 11 students. Belarus used to have Grade 12 but got rid of it as a cost-saving measure. After Grade 11 there, kids can start to work or go to university or technical college. The girls looked like prom girls everywhere: each girl wore a fancy dress, her hair was made up, and she looked very elegant. You couldn't tell them apart from Western girls. The boys wore suits and ties, but they were obviously cheaply made (some were velour), and the material soaked up the water. The boys looked too young to graduate.

After a break, the graduates, their families, the teachers, and our little group from Canada were seated in the town cinema for continued festivities. Teachers spoke, graduates were called up one by one and congratulated, but mostly the graduating class entertained us. Some sang, some danced, some played instruments. The class sang many songs together, with each student taking a solo part. It was well choreographed and well rehearsed. It was a wonderful show, and all of us thought that the graduates must have spent at least half a year preparing for it. So, in addition to losing a year of schooling, they lost another half year of studies practising for their graduation.

No one asked us "Who are you?" They all knew. Djatlovo is an isolated town and rarely gets foreigners. We were the first foreigners ever invited to a graduation ceremony, and we were asked to give a speech. Luckily for me, I was jet lagged (lucky in only one sense) and awake in the middle of the night, so I could write my speech. The whole speech is below. I delivered it with pauses for translation, and though it was kind of heavy, compared with the rest of the two-and-a-half-hour indoor program, people listened politely, and I was presented with flowers at the end of my speech.

This type of graduation could not have taken place in Canada or the United States. It was a throwback to more naive times, kind of like stepping through the television set into the movie *Pleasantville*. But we enjoyed it immensely, and it gave us a taste of small-town Belarus life. My Djatlovo graduation class remarks follow.

It is a great thrill and honour for me to speak to these distinguished graduation classes on behalf of my family. I knew I would attend this ceremony, so I packed my best suit and tie from Canada to have here today. Unfortunately, the airline made different travel arrangements for me than for my luggage, and I arrived in Djatlovo the day my suitcase arrived in Warsaw.

I would like to speak briefly about two topics, one being history and the second being tolerance. But first I want to congratulate each graduate here today; you have succeeded in reaching a very important milestone in your lives, and I commend you and wish you every success.

It seems to me that everything we learn can be related to history, but we don't always realize it. In science, it is clear that in order to advance one must learn from what has gone before. New creations are built on prior knowledge and result in new medicines, new products, and new technologies so that all of our lives are improved. That is a form of learning from history.

In world events, and in our daily lives, I believe it is just as important to learn from history. It has been said many times that, if one does not learn the lessons of history, one is bound to make the same mistakes that were made before. And when you study history, there is no better place to start than in your own home city and then expand to your region, your country, and the world.

That brings me to my second point, that of tolerance. The history of Djatlovo teaches us very clearly that intolerance leads to terrible suffering and destruction. The people of Djatlovo suffered under occupation for many years by rulers who treated some people differently from others just because of their religion or their culture, and that led to disaster.

And when I talk about the people of Djatlovo, I say our people, my people, because I don't know how many generations of my own family were born and lived here, but I do know that my father and his brother and sisters and their parents all lived here, and maybe many generations before them, and they were happy here until Nazis came here intent on murder.

When my father's family lived here, they lived in harmony with their neighbours even though they were Jewish and many of their neighbours were Orthodox or Catholic. Their differences did not matter. People of Djatlovo then knew that all people want the same basic things: to live their lives in security and freedom, to keep their dignity, and to have the same opportunities as everyone else without discrimination.

Being a member of one religion or culture is just one way to live your life: it is not better or worse than anyone else's way; it is the way you have chosen. Your religion, your culture, your language, your country, these are choices you make for yourself, and you should be proud of them. But they do not make you better or worse than anyone else on this earth.

My father, Rubin Pinsky, and my cousin Lawrence's father, Herzl Pinsky, whose pictures hang in your very moving and informative Holocaust museum, had to fight for this country because of the hatred of others, my father as a partisan and my uncle in the Red Army. May none of us ever need to go through what they survived.

You students here in Djatlovo are much luckier than most. You have had teachers and supportive schools, including our friends Zhanna Nagavonskaya, Yelena Abramchik, and many others, who have taught you some of these very important lessons. I hope that you graduates can see that good work, like the work that resulted in the creation of two museums of history at your high school, can have an important effect not only on people in your own town but also on people around the world. Our family have come from Canada, 12,000 kilometres away, because what people have done in Djatlovo affects us profoundly.

Our wish for each graduating student is that each of you strives to do at least one good thing for your people and your country and that you too can make a difference. Dzakui.

*

JUNE 12, 2012

From the Beginning

It's time to catch up on what we have actually been doing since we started our journey into Belarus, which was only six days ago but seems like an emotional lifetime. On Thursday, June 7, we took a train from central Warsaw to Terespol, on the Polish side of the border with Belarus. We met our fixer, Yuri, who guided us through the border crossing. From Canada, one does not think of border crossings as a very big deal, but this border is *really* a big deal because it separates the European Union from the Russian bloc. Belarus is really a proxy state of Russia, and there are no border customs or stops from Belarus to anywhere in Russia. Just like in the European Union, you see a sign and by that know you are in a different country. The European Union has free flow of goods among countries, and Russia does not. There is an incredible amount of smuggling going on from Poland into Belarus since prices are cheaper and goods much more numerous and varied in the European Union than in Russia. One other point: Belarus charges a 60-euro entrance fee for a visa for each entry of a foreigner and the same charge for Belarusians who leave to the European Union. This greatly discourages tourism, so there are very few tourists here. It is not the kind of place you look for tourist information; there is none possibly in the whole country. As I write that, I ask myself "What have we gotten ourselves into?"

The train between Terespol in Poland and Brest in Belarus took 15 minutes. The cars were made of wood and probably over 50 years old. Terespol and Brest are a few kilometres apart, and the ride was 15 minutes at a slow speed. We then got out for customs inspection. The train systems are completely different in Russia from the European Union, with the rails and therefore the wheel axles being wider in Russia than in the European Union or the rest of the world. When in the former Soviet Union, you travel Russian style or not at all. Yuri handed us our Belarus medical insurance policies required to get into the country; he told us that if something happened to us we would have to rely on our foreign medical insurance; this was just another entry tax called by another name. It was cheap, but we started to realize that our way of thinking was simply not going to work in Belarus, a realization that has been confirmed many times over in the past five days.

Yuri warned us that border guards are snarly and would ask us how much cash we have (he told us to bring euros and US dollars because there are very few places that accept credit cards) and that, if we have a lot (e.g., over $3,000), they would give us a hard time. We braced ourselves for the worst, but with the customs agents unable to communicate with us to ask questions they did not give us much hassle. They did open our luggage, and for me it was a breeze, my luggage still being in Warsaw.

We spent a few hours walking in Brest and having lunch. Brest is best known as the place where Hitler and Stalin made their famous Brest-Litovsk treaty in 1939, dividing up Poland between them. That is why the border is there now, because what Hitler took is now modern Poland, and what Stalin took is now modern Belarus. The Soviet side really became "Russified" in 1939.

From Brest, we took a surprisingly modern train for two hours to Ivatsevichy. The train is called the Swiss Train because of its sleek and new appearance. Ivatsevichy is where Zhanna K (described in my post entitled "The Saints of Belarus") lives, but we didn't stop there. We met our driver for Belarus, Misha, and drove straight to Djatlovo. We have been driving around in Misha's extra-large van ever since.

We were met by Zhanna Nagavonskaya at the Djatlovo hotel and had a late dinner with her. We call her *our* Zhanna because Max had met her over three years earlier, and I had been in correspondence with her. We started to learn about her work on Holocaust remembrance. I had been in correspondence with her using Google Translate, but it doesn't do a great job of translation. To be able to talk to her through our incredibly knowledgeable and talented interpreter, Yuri, was a treat. We got the first feeling for what a saint she was. We went to sleep in awe that we were there, in the town of our father and grandparents, a place that I never thought I would get to. It was like a dream and a nightmare come true at the same time.

On Friday morning, we drove back to Ivatsevichy to meet Zhanna K, and she took us to Kosava (formerly called Kosov Poleski) so that we could see the memorial to the 2,800 Jews slaughtered in one spot in 1942. This monument was put up only because of Zhanna K's perseverance. It is in a small clearing in the forest. She also took us to see the remains of the Jewish cemetery, where the only evidence that can be seen of its history are gravestones dug out of the ground by grave robbers. Although the grave robbers had bad intentions, they actually uncovered gravestones that otherwise would be buried and forgotten. The robbers didn't get anything for their efforts, for Jews never bury anything valuable with a corpse.

Kosava is of particular importance to Lawrence because that is where my grandparents sent his father, my uncle Herzl, to live with his uncle Leib when Herzl was about eight years old. He spent over eight years there, and Leib became like a father to him. Whereas the trip by car today is an hour and 20 minutes on the highway, in the 1930s it was more than a day's journey by horse and buggy. My father, Rubin, Herzl's younger brother, told me that he went to Kosava once to see his brother after not seeing him for over three years.

The spot where 2,800 Kosava Jews were murdered in one night was probably the place where Leib and his wife met their end. We said Kaddish for them and for the 2,798 others who rest there, may they rest in peace.

There were six of us Pinskys travelling, and each time we came to a memorial site or a cemetery we said Kaddish together. It is a prayer for the dead extolling God's virtues. There is no mention of death or the dead person. It is a mitzvah, or a "good deed," to say Kaddish for members of your immediate family at specific times, but it is also a mitzvah to say Kaddish for people for whom there is no one left to say it. We performed a lot of mitzvahs, and we felt redeemed for it. On the one hand, with so many murdered, Hitler came close to exterminating the Jews of Europe. On the other hand, here we are, in the killing fields of Europe, saying Kaddish for all those souls.

To me, this experience gives a new meaning not only to life and its gifts, for sure, but also to life's responsibilities. Maybe life is a long lesson in learning to appreciate and accept them both.

*

JUNE 13, 2012

Be Still, My Heart

Saturday, June 9, 2012, was certainly among the most emotional days of my life. It was later that day that we attended the Djatlovo high school graduation and I delivered a speech, which I blogged about previously. It was the morning of that day that brought me to tears.

Zhanna met us after breakfast for a walk to Kurpishiwald, the place in the nearby forest where 2,800 Jewish older people and children were murdered on April 30, 1942. Those Jews were rounded up from their small ghetto in Djatlovo just before dawn. They were told that they were to be moved to better quarters not far away, to leave everything behind, since they could come back for their belongings later.

The road to Kurpishiwald was about two kilometres and lined with some houses in the first few blocks. The people in those houses were warned by the Nazis to get inside and lock the doors. They were also ordered to block their windows facing the road with pillows. As the Jews started their march, some of them realized what was going to happen, but they had no strength left to fight. Some shouted as they passed their neighbours' houses, telling their friends that they could keep a watch or some kitchen appliance left in their houses or saying their goodbyes. Others hung on to the belief that the Nazis had told them the truth.

We walked along the same route as our relatives had, though knowing that we would be walking back to Djatlovo alive. Zhanna told us the stories that she had collected about that morning as we walked, bringing the terror of that 1942 dawn to 2012. At the site, a memorial plaque was affixed to a dignified stone column in front of a mound, about 10 metres wide and 40 metres long. The mound contained 2,800 bodies, and witnesses who dared to approach it the next day said that the thin layer of earth covering the bodies writhed for days from the struggles of the not yet dead. Rumour had it that one child actually lived by being covered with bodies, and he waited until everyone left to crawl out.

Our grandparents, Baruch Lippa Pinsky, for whom I am named, his wife, Henya, for whom my sister, Helen, is named, and their 10-year-old daughter, Rachel, for whom Max's daughter, Rachael, is named, were among those murdered that day. We stood in front of the memorial for a long time and thought about our relatives who had died at that spot, and we said Kaddish, the most meaningful ever. We then walked back to town, mostly in silence.

The afternoon was no less of a strain on our hearts but in a good way. We went to the high school where Zhanna teaches, and we were treated to a visit first to its history museum featuring various ethnic groups and then to its annexed room of the Holocaust. The main museum is an attempt to teach children about diversity and women's rights in addition to history. The Holocaust display is in a separate, tiny room, but it is well done. The first small panel of about one metre in width shows pictures of Jewish life before the Second World War. There are some small artifacts of Jewish life, including a Hannukah candelabra, Shabbat candlesticks, and so on. The next panel has pictures of Jewish groups who posed for them, such as political clubs and school graduates. Then there is a panel with well-known pictures of Nazi atrocities, none of which was taken in Djatlovo, but they get the message across (e.g., the iconic picture of a Nazi pointing his rifle at a small child with his hands up).

The next panel is a wall painting with a blue background and thousands of yellow stars ascending like smoke. The symbolism is clear. That wall faces the door. On the right-side wall are representations of a few survivors of the Holocaust. There is a string of Israeli flags along the top of the wall, above everything else. There are a few pictures of people from Djatlovo who survived the war, and, to our astonishment, in a frame by itself, are four pictures of my father, my uncle, and their two sisters (though only one sister survived). This was a complete surprise to us. There, in a tiny museum half a world away, my father's memory is kept alive by complete strangers. And above their pictures is a picture of Max and his daughter, Rachael, from three years ago. It was a powerful symbol of generations continuing even after tragic events.

There is also a world map as part of the Holocaust display. The whole right side of the room is intended to show that there is still Jewish life even after the Holocaust and that the descendants of the Jews of Djatlovo now live all over the world.

This little town honours my family, and we didn't know it until then. In a sense, we were being honoured simply for caring about and showing interest in our past, but mostly our parents were being honoured for just having survived. Until I went to Djatlovo, I'm not sure that I fully appreciated what an incredible accomplishment that was.

*

JUNE 15, 2012

There Was Resistance

The Nazis were clever in how over time they broke down the will of their victims to resist, taking away more and more of their dignity (Jews cannot be teachers, cannot attend school, cannot work for the government, cannot touch food served to non-Jews), their implements of potential resistance (guns, knives, silverware confiscated), their financial wherewithal (furs, jewellery, cash confiscated), and their physical strength (small rations, backbreaking slave labour) so that the victims had no strength and no will left. In addition, leaders of Jewish communities were taken away first and told that they would be resettled, but most often they were killed, so there were no acknowledged community leaders left. Yet there was resistance, the most well known being the Warsaw Ghetto Uprising (read Leon Uris's book *Mila 18*) and the Bielski brothers partisan group (see the movie *Defiance*). In the end, the leadership of the Jewish resistance fell to people in their 20s who had been raised to become craftsmen or teachers but had never handled a gun or been leaders of anything.

On Sunday, June 10, we learned of another incredible instance of resistance. Novogrudok is an unexceptional town in most ways, except that since 2008 it has housed a museum of Jewish resistance as one of the town's three museums, a high number for a population of 12,000. The resistance museum was created and is run by Tamara Vershitskaya, the director of all three museums in town and an expert on its history. She became fascinated with the story of the daring escape of 252 Jews from the Novogrudok work camp.

In 1941, the Nazis put 6,000 of Novogrudok's Jews (out of a total population of almost 10,000) into a small ghetto, squeezing 60 people into each small house. In taking information about each person (the Nazis kept immaculate records), they found out that a huge number of the Jews were tradesmen and artisans. The town had been known for metal forging, carpentry, watchmaking, and so on. So the Nazis separated about 1,000 tradesmen to use for slave labour and support their war effort and put them into a building next to the town courthouse. The other 5,000 Jews were murdered within six months of Nazi rule.

One would think that it would be important to the Nazis to keep their slave labourers reasonably healthy in order to help the war effort, but it was more important than anything else for the Nazis to kill Jews. They gave the tradesmen one slice of bread a day and some watery potato soup. That was it. Naturally, as they weakened, the slaves' output was reduced. Those who didn't die of hunger were killed as punishment for not performing.

Unknown to the Nazis, these carpenters and metalworkers were working for the Nazis during the day and working on their escape during the night. It is absolutely unbelievable that they could do it, but these starved slaves dug a tunnel from their barracks 200 metres to the forest. The tunnel was one metre beneath the ground and just big enough for skinny people to crawl through it. The earth dug for the tunnel was stored in the ceiling of their barracks, so the ceiling had to be reinforced immensely to support all that weight. The tunnel was ready in 1943, and there were three false starts since conditions weren't right to flee for one reason or another. On the date in 1943 when they decided to go, the leaders of the tunnel builders forced all of the remaining prisoners but six into the tunnel. The six who didn't go hid from the others in the earth above the ceiling. They were claustrophobic and knew that they would panic in the tunnel and probably give everyone else away.

Into the tunnel went 252 people, many of them thinking that they would suffocate underground. There was little air for 252 people squeezed into 200 metres of tunnel. Some very small reeds were used as air vents along the route, small enough that they wouldn't be seen from the ground above. People almost asphyxiated, yet miraculously no one died in the tunnel. There was a snag at the tunnel exit, and it took 15 minutes for the first crawlers to get it open, but finally it did open.

As the people came out and stood up in the fresh air, both it and their sudden standing after the heat and little air of the tunnel resulted in many of them becoming dizzy and disoriented. Some started running in the wrong direction, toward the camp instead of into the forest. The guards, who had been plied with alcohol as gifts to ensure that they would be drunk and less perceptive to noises or strange goings on, even in their drunken state heard some noise, saw prisoners outside the barracks, and started shooting. Some of the escapees were killed that way, but the vast majority did escape into the forest. Those who did joined the Bielski partisan brigade stationed not far away.

The Germans went into the barracks the next morning, found the tunnel, concluded that everyone had escaped, and over the following week pulled out all the equipment and anything else valuable and then abandoned the building. On the eighth day after the escape, the six people who had hid in the earth above the ceiling simply came down and walked out of the empty camp. They ran to the forest, found the Bielskis, and survived the war.

The site of the Jewish resistance museum in Novogrudok is the barracks of those escapees, and the tunnel opening is its central attraction. People who actually took part in the escape funded the museum's creation. In October 2012, an Israeli film director is going to Novogrudok to film a documentary on this miraculous escape. Today there are three escapees still alive, one in Israel and two in the United States.

We were invited to attend the filming of the documentary, and I know that it would be an incredible experience, but I also know that I won't be able to make a trip like this again, certainly not so soon after this experience. This one short week has been an emotional decade. We finally got wifi, and I checked a few work emails last night: has time really stood still while we have travelled for years here in Eastern Europe? Maybe when I get back to Canada it will still be June 2012, but right now that seems incredible to me.

*

JUNE 16, 2012

Lviv, Lvov, Lemberg

We took a night train from Pinsk to Lviv, crossing from Belarus into Ukraine. The train was great: we had sleeping rooms where two narrow bunk beds slept four people. The rocking of the train lulled us to sleep quickly each time the noise or a whistle stop woke us up. We arrived in Lviv at about 6 a.m. The border required two stops, one on each side, and though the border police like to appear threatening (one customs agent told us to open all our bags but was overruled by another agent) it went reasonably smoothly.

This marked the official end of the roots trip on my father's side and started the roots trip on my mother's side. Although the town that her parents came from is very similar to that of my father, and though 800 kilometres apart, at times they were both part of Poland. But there is a world of difference for us. My mother's parents immigrated to Canada in 1926, well before the Second World War. They lost many relatives in the war, but my grandparents were safe, and my mother was born in Canada. Nonetheless, this portion of our trip was no less meaningful.

Lviv is the Ukrainian name for the city, it was Lvov under the Soviets, and in German it is known as Lemberg. My mother's parents lived there for five years, and though they were quite poor they hosted a number of their close relatives in their house, sometimes for a year or more at a time. This house was where my late uncle Sam Moser spent his early childhood and where my mother's late cousin Shia spent a year with my grandparents while going to school. It was a thrill to find the little house and take pictures, and we realized later that they occupied only half of what we thought was already a small place. But they were poor, and this was how they lived. Others in our family who lived in Lviv include Izzie Moser, born there, and Freda Thau, both of whom are known to some of the readers of this blog.

My grandfather Menachem Mendel, for whom my brother, Max, is named, bought leather in Krakow and resold it in

Lviv to shoemakers from 1921 to 1925. Business was not good, and my grandfather was thought to be a poor businessman. Although the business went bankrupt in 1925, that turned out not to be the case. Ironically, it was the failure of his business that saved his family's lives. He asked his brother Robert Moser, who had immigrated to Canada in 1923, to sponsor him for immigration. My grandfather thought that he needed a fresh start. One sign that we read in Lviv stated that, of the city's Jewish population of 110,000 in 1939, only 800 survived the Holocaust. Ironic again in that my grandfather, later with his son Sam's help, started and built up a western shirt-manufacturing business in Winnipeg called Mid-West Garments, and it eventually had over 300 employees. He was not such a bad businessman after all.

We spent the first morning in Lviv with the American Joint Distribution Committee (JDC, to which I have donated), and we were shown its *chesed* building. *Chesed* means "an act of charity," and that is exactly what happens in the building. The JDC concentrates on providing services to both the young and the elderly. With regard to the young, it takes in children from two to six years old from families in crisis (alcoholic parents, children with mental disabilities, etc.) and provides preschool and kindergarten programs from 10 a.m. to 5:30 p.m. five days a week, including a hot meal and snacks. For the elderly, the JDC runs programs aimed at getting isolated people together, such as knitting projects, singing together, playing chess, and offering dance lessons to the fittest of them. The seniors have snacks together, and it is the highlight of the week for the six groups of about 20 people each. Each group meets once every two weeks. The JDC also provides trained social workers for those in need. We were told that until five years ago there were no social workers in all of Ukraine since social work wasn't taught at any Ukrainian university. The JDC operates all over the former Soviet Union, and it does incredible work.

Lviv is a nice city, with people telling us that it should be considered in the same category as Budapest or Prague. I have been to both of those cities in the past five years, and though Lviv does have some lovely buildings from the 17th and 18th centuries, and some nice (but uneven) cobblestone streets, it is simply too shabby to put into the same category as those world-class cities. It is also very disorganized. For example, when a road is a bit wider than just two narrow lanes, people park in the middle of it facing both ways so that each lane of moving cars has a sidewalk on the right (often filled with parked cars as well as pedestrians) and parked cars on the left. Crazy.

We stayed in a three-bedroom apartment on the third floor of a building that was at least 100 years old, and that was when they probably last refurnished the place, for $375 per night. We were lucky to get it: it was comfortable, and because of the Euro 2012 soccer championships many hotel rooms were going for $1,000. More on Euro 2012 in my next posting.

*

JUNE 16, 2012

Euro Cup 2012

The big event in Poland and Ukraine while we were visiting was the soccer championship of Europe, called Euro Cup 2012. It was both a good and a bad thing for us. On the one hand, Ukraine, which does not usually have many tourists, was ready for thousands of Western tourists, and many airport, hotel, and security workers learned a few basic words of English to accommodate visitors. On the other hand, some places in Ukraine jacked up prices to gouge the foreigners. It wasn't like that in Poland. The Polish didn't seem to get too greedy since they are used to EU travellers, but prices in Warsaw are not much lower than those in Western Europe anyway. We also benefited from the strength of the US dollar compared with the euro during this euro-zone crisis.

Max was able to secure four tickets to a Euro Cup game in Lviv, matching Denmark against Portugal. Daniella graciously permitted the four guys to go: Simon, Max, Yuri, and me. The game was exciting, won by a very talented Portugal team 3-2. It was great to be at a match. There were far more Danish fans, we reckoned, because they can better afford to travel than Portuguese fans. One thing that surprised us was that there were Carlsberg beer tents all over selling beer, and of course we bought a pint each. After drinking it, we realized that there was no alcohol in the beer. Since there were no other beer vendors, and no drinks were let in anywhere near the stadium, the crowd was a lot less rowdy than it otherwise might have been. It just was good, clean fun, and I couldn't help thinking that playoff hockey games in Vancouver could learn a thing or two there.

One exception to the fun was the march of 1,000 Russian fans in Warsaw the day of the game between Russia and Poland. It resulted in some fights, but it was like waving a red flag in front of a bull, for the Russians are not well liked in either Poland or Ukraine. Russian tourists are like former ugly Americans, loud and brash and arrogant. They are hated in Ukraine because Ukrainians have not forgotten how the Soviets nationalized their farms starting in 1919 to turn them into collective farms. Most Ukrainians at the time were farmers, and, as we previously learned in former Yugoslavia, people in

Eastern Europe simply will not forgive and forget, even if they don't get to take their revenge for five or six generations.

Oh, the Russia-Poland game? Russia spanked Poland, much to local chagrin!

Each city hosting games, and I believe there are eight of them, has a huge fan zone of several square blocks with huge screens and fake beer. Thousands who want to watch the games together can gather there, and they do. Unlike Vancouver's fan zones during the Olympics, there are dozens of entry and exit points, so we didn't have to wait in long queues to get in. Those in the fan zones, like those at the game that we attended, were very well behaved. The two soccer stadiums that we saw, Lviv's from the inside and Warsaw's on the outside, both looked new. Like many major sporting events, Euro 2012 was a big boost to the Polish and Ukrainian economies. Ukraine needs that boost and a lot more.

*

JUNE 16, 2012

Roots, Ukrainian Style

Our group's last full day together was Thursday, June 14. As we started the day, 20-year-old Simon said that he was "all Jewed out." I knew what he meant, and I was starting to feel the same way. It had been a very intense 10 days so far, and we realized that our lives are much more like everyone else's in Canada compared with the segregated Jewish lives that our ancestors lived in Eastern Europe. Even so, our grandparents on our mother's side were much more modern and assimilated than our father's family. Our maternal grandfather, Menachem Mendel, was drafted into the Austro-Hungarian army in the First World War and fought at that time on the Russian front until he was captured in 1915. Miraculously, he escaped from captivity and hid in Chertkov, the "big" town (perhaps 10,000 people) only seven kilometres from his hometown of Jagielnica for about a year so that he wouldn't be sent to the front again. He knew that if he returned to the front, he would never return home.

We learned in Lviv that Jews made up over 20 percent of the officers in the Austro-Hungarian army in the First World War. They were very loyal to Kaiser Franz-Joseph because he was tolerant of all his subjects' religions. Jews and other religious minorities thrived under his rule, but ironically this led to their being lulled into inaction in the Second World War. Because the Austrian kaisers were Germanic, the Jews of the former Austro-Hungarian Empire did not fear the Nazis as much as they should have. Even the wealthy people in this region who perhaps could have escaped after Germany took over Austria in 1938 did not do so. They thought that the Jewish community knew the Germans well and had proven their loyalty over many decades, so they believed that they didn't have much to fear. By the time they realized their mistake, it was too late.

As an example, in Jagielnica, where we can trace at least six generations of Mosers (my mother's maiden name) from 1790, all 1,300 Jews of the town were assembled in a town school and shot. We learned from a local woman (described below) that three people survived, two of them children aged four and seven. They were hidden by their mother in a cornfield just before the roundup. Days after the massacre, the farm woman who owned the field saw that some ears of corn had been eaten raw. When she investigated, she heard crying. She saved the children and treated them as her own throughout the remainder of the war.

It is not an easy journey from Lviv to Jagielnica. We could have hired a driver to take us the 200-plus kilometres, but the roads are very poor. Instead, we took an early two-hour train ride from Lviv to Ternopol and hired a driver from there. It took another hour and a half to get to Jagielnica via Chertkov. We had been warned that there was nothing in Jagielnica, and that is true of buildings that existed before the Second World War, but it is not true of the town itself. There was a pretty good restaurant in the town where we lunched on freshly made borscht and perogies. There was also a museum in this town of about 2,000 people, and the local "curator" gave us a guided tour of the four small rooms.

When the curator learned that we were interested in the Jewish history of the town (after all, it had been 95 percent Jewish), he concentrated on the picture of the town circa 1910, pretty much the only indication in the museum that there had been a Jewish presence. Every building in that picture was owned and inhabited by Jews or was a Jewish shop. Not a single building from that picture remains. After all the Jews were killed, the area farmers did not want to move into town; they wanted to stay on their land. Clay and wood buildings rotted and fell. Stones from the sturdier buildings were hauled 80 kilometres to rebuild the city of Ternopol.

When the curator found out that our ancestors were from the town, he wanted to know the family name, but it wasn't familiar to him. He said that there was someone in town, though, who might remember our family. We visited with a short, wizened, and wrinkled woman who looked 100 but we calculated would be 80. She was in Grade 3 in 1941 and remembered many Jewish families but not the Mosers. She told us the story of the end of the town's Jews and the two children who survived. The third Jewish survivor of the town, away at the time of the roundup, had died two years before our visit. There was no one else in the town old enough to remember the war. We had arrived in time to talk to the last person who remembered, and we were thankful for that.

We visited one more, somewhat bigger, town about 15 kilometres from Jagielnica called Tluste, where we knew Mosers had lived, but we didn't know how or even whether those Mosers were related. There was a museum there, too, and though the curator didn't know our Moser name there was a memorial outside the town created with funding from about 20 families from the United States and Israel, and four of those families were named Moser. Also in the museum were pictures from the early 20th century, and they showed townspeople of all faiths mingling and celebrating events together.

On the way back from Tluste through Jagielnica, we decided to say Kaddish beside the building where the 1,300 Jews died. A man saw us and came over. He offered to let us download the town's 20 or so pictures from before the Second World War from the town's computer archives. Ever-resourceful Yuri had a thumb drive on him, so we did, including the picture of the town discussed above. I know that others in the Moser clan will be interested in getting copies of these pictures. The curator also made us promise to send him pictures of Mosers who lived in Jagielnica to add to the town's meagre picture collection.

After the drive back to Ternopol and the train back to Lviv, it was almost 10 p.m. Almost all restaurants in Lviv close at 10 p.m. A taxi took us to the only restaurant in this city of 350,000 people that stays open until midnight, and we had our farewell meal. We dined on a traditional Carpathian fare of pickles, pickled salad, and as a main course what could only be described as cream of wheat with mushrooms, chased down by several bottles of vodka. It was surprisingly decent. We said our goodbyes to my brother and nephew, without whose initiative I would never have embarked on this adventure. Max and Simon left the apartment at 5 a.m. to catch their flight to Kiev and then London.

*

My Book Served Its Purpose

A purpose you impart is no longer your own.
—Johann Wolfgang von Goethe (1749–1832), German poet, novelist, and dramatist

The most unfortunate aspect of not getting my luggage until my roots trip was over was that I was unable to give some of the gifts that I had brought from Canada. What do you give to a righteous person doing something to preserve the memory of my people and my family while living in a country where nobody else cares to know about the past? I knew exactly what to give, and I searched through all the Judaica shops in Vancouver and then Seattle to no avail, but I found the perfect gifts in "Israel's Judaica" shop in Toronto. In my view, the perfect gift is a Hanukiah, the nine-candle candelabra used to celebrate Hanukah, the Jewish festival of light. Each day for eight days candles are lit, starting with two candles and ending with nine candles on the last day, so that more and more light is brought into the home as the holiday goes on. I bought two exquisite Swarovski-style Hanukiahs, simple but with gems embedded in them, very elegant looking. I also bought two Hanukiahs made by Gary Rosenthal of Los Angeles, and they were like heavy silver bars with a ceramic front and holes in the width part for the candles. Finally, I bought two small brass oil lamp Hanukiahs, which burn oil with a wick. I even bought special candles and oil wicks.

I packed the Swarovski Hanukiahs and the oil Hanukiahs in my suitcase but decided to take the Rosenthals in my carry-on bag because they were quite heavy, and I was worried that my suitcase would be overweight. Man, was that lucky! In the end, we had the two Rosenthals to give to the two Zhannas, and we said the same thing to both of them: the Hanukiah represents the light that you have brought to your own people through your imparting of knowledge and history, the light that you have brought to our family through your caring, and most importantly the light that you have brought to the memory of those who perished in the Holocaust. I hope that each found the gift as meaningful as it was intended to be.

Someone whom we spent a lot of time with in Djatlovo besides Zhanna was Yelena Abramchik, another high school teacher of the Russian Orthodox faith instrumental in creating the two history museums in the Djatlovo high school. She is also a part-time journalist, and she edited excerpts of my book in Russian for publication in the Belarus Jewish monthly newspaper. She admired my father for his ability to keep getting up and starting his life again after each adversity, something that I hope came through in my book. Yelena invited us to her home for dinner and was wonderful to us. I was sorry not to be able to give her a beautiful Swarovski or Rosenthal Hanukiah. Yuri told us not to try to ship or mail it to Belarus, for the recipient would be hit with crippling import duties, even on a small item such as Hanukah candles. The small oil lamp Hanukiahs would have been perfect gifts for the museums in Jagielnica and Tluste in Ukraine. As things stood, we gave the curators the usual gift in Eastern Europe, a bottle of decent booze. That is how things are done there.

We didn't talk with Zhanna or Yelena much about my "manuscriptella" (see the blog post "My Book: It's not Fair!" for the definition of that word) about my father, and it wasn't part of the Holocaust exhibit in Djatlovo or even referred to there. I realized that this was completely fitting: it is not a scholarly work, not a reference book, and was written from second-hand memories. I had written it in 1996 to honour my father, and it has been an incredible bonus that it has provided us with a strong link to the place where my father and his family lived. It has more than served its purpose. Now I even have a disk with a Word version of the "manuscriptella" in Russian, and I hope to put that on the internet soon.

The flights home—Warsaw to London, London to Edmonton, Edmonton to Vancouver—were uneventful, and all the luggage arrived when and where it should. Both Daniella and I had a renewed appreciation for Canada as soon as we got to Edmonton: even the agent as we cleared customs smiled and was helpful to us, never mind others whom we asked questions of or ticket agents who changed our seats. People *smile* here, they provide service as if they *want* to help, and that is so different from Eastern Europe. We live in a great, great country, and we will never forget that.

Some pictures of our trip for those who are interested are in the last three posts of my blog site, rootstrip.wordpress.com.

PART III

The Tailor Project

I don't remember exactly what alerted me to it, but sometime in the first half of 2018 I was notified that someone in Toronto was trying to get in touch with the relatives of all those Jews who had arrived in Canada as tailors as part of a Canadian government recruiting project in the European displaced person (DP) camps after the Second World War. Perhaps it was an ad in Vancouver's *Jewish Independent* weekly newspaper. I called the number listed and spoke to Nicole Bryck, who explained that she was a researcher helping Larry Enkin, the son of Toronto clothing manufacturer Max Enkin. Max was one of the Jewish manufacturers in Toronto who initiated a project to bring to Canada Holocaust survivors stranded in DP camps in Europe.

I told Nicole about the manuscript that I had written about my father, which I later sent to her, and I told her about Rubin and Harry and how they had arrived in Canada in early 1948. I later spent an hour on the phone with Nicole and Larry telling them the story of Rubin and Harry as described in Part I of this book. They listened politely, Larry clearly enjoying hearing about the lives of more Jews whom his father had been instrumental in bringing to Canada.

From Nicole, I got a copy of the USS *General S.D. Sturgis* passenger list for the voyage that Rubin and Harry were on and learned that it had docked in Halifax on January 13, 1948.

I learned that at that time they spelled their last name Pinski, not Pinsky, though that might have been how the immigration officials chose to spell it when they heard it pronounced. Harry was officially listed as Hercel. I learned that Rubin and Harry were listed by the ship's documents as having come from the Bucholz DP camp, not from Bergen Belsen, where they were living, and I have no idea why. The two DP camps were over 50 kilometres apart. From Nicole, I also received a page from the "Report on Displaced Person Tailors" from the files of the Canadian Overseas Garment Commission. It is not dated, but likely it was compiled in 1949 or 1950. An image of the page is included in the photographs section of this book. Hercel Pinski was listed as being employed by Standard Cloak at 1470 Peel Street, Montreal, and Rubin Pinski's "present employer" was listed as "Seminary" with no address indicated.

The book *The Tailor Project: How 2,500 Holocaust Survivors Found a New Life in Canada*, by Andrea Knight, Paula Draper, and Nicole Bryck (Toronto: Second Story Press, 2020), details how Canada's Jewish community led by garment manufacturers was able to cause the first cracks in Canada's horribly anti-Jewish immigration policies and bring Jewish Holocaust survivors living in Europe's DP camps to Canada for the first time. Because Rubin and Harry came to Canada under the Canadian Garment Workers Scheme, its origin is of particular interest to me and to the story of my father, so it is relevant to include at least a summary of it here. Since *The Tailor Project* tells those stories so well, I will quote from it so that readers of *Ordinary, Extraordinary* can understand that Rubin and Harry were able to come to Canada only thanks to the dedication and perseverance of others. My summary is no substitute for reading the *The Tailor Project*, which tells the life stories and societal contributions of some of the immigrants admitted under the Canadian Garment Workers Scheme.

With the permission of Second Story Press, the following offsets are quotations with page references from *The Tailor Project*. I have added some words in brackets to give the quotations proper contexts. I recommend this well-researched book to anyone interested in learning more about Canada's history of discrimination against Jewish immigration and about some of the rescued Jewish people who lived full lives and contributed to Canada thanks in part to the hard work and perseverance of Max Enkin and others.

> The 1948–1949 Garment Workers Scheme owes its beginnings to the Canadian Jewish Congress, the Jewish Labour Committee, and all the participating actors—firms, unions, and community organizations—who worked together to make the project possible.... Larry Enkin, Max Enkin's son, grew up hearing stories from his father about the Garment Workers Scheme. Sixty-five years later he asked the important questions: Where are those tailors today? What is their story? How did these survivors contribute to Canada? (1–2)
>
> If Canada [in 1946] was to progress on the world stage, it would need to revitalize the economy. It was becoming clear that the road to prosperity would have to be built with the help of immigrant workers. This would require a drastic overhaul of the policies. (9)
>
> It had been decades since Canadian immigration officials had worked to admit applicants rather than bar them. Although their instructions were to screen solely for "subversives," they made it clear ... that Jews would be refused. When the first group of 1,700 [recruited

labourers] arrived in Canada, it included a single Jew. There were only three Jews among the 2,900 who had arrived by 1947.... By 1947, Canada had increased its quota to admit 20,000 DPs by the middle of the following year.... Although these schemes were in principle open to everyone in the camps, the reality was that the ethnic stereotypes restricted many from these programs. (19)

Young, unmarried Jewish survivors were more than willing to find a way out of the camps by applying for Canadian labour schemes. Many Jewish women had experience in nursing care in hospitals after liberation. Most were rejected outright: those who were initially approved found their security clearances retracted after cables were received from Ottawa drawing a line against Jews. None of this was announced publicly, although it was clearly noted by shocked International Refugee Organization officials. (20)

Joe Salsberg, ... member of the Ontario legislature, travelled to Europe in the fall of 1947 on a private fact-finding mission....[H]e reported [about Canadian immigration officers] ... "while in some cases it is concealed, discrimination is brazen and unashamed in others."... In one case, eleven Jewish men who had passed all the tests and screening for the forestry program had their visas taken from them at the last minute. In another, he described how every Jewish woman in one camp who applied for the domestic [worker] scheme was rejected, except for one, who listed herself as a "Polish Christian." Salsberg wrote that the vice consuls "insist on the listing of Jewish immigrants as of the 'Hebrew' race. They showed me forms on which they scratched out the 'White' designation and imposed 'Hebrew' instead." (20–21)

The horrifying news of the Kielce pogrom in Poland in July 1946 shocked Canadian Jewry. The murder of forty-two and wounding of fifty concentration camp survivors by their neighbours prompted a massive exodus from Poland.... The bulk labour programs initiated by the Canadian government had not gone unnoticed by the JLC [Jewish Labour Committee], by Jewish clothing manufacturers, or by the CJC [Canadian Jewish Congress]. (51)

The organized Jewish community had pursued almost two decades of quiet diplomacy in their rescue attempts with very little to show for it.... All three groups saw the bulk labour schemes as a model for the entry of at least a portion of the surviving remnant [of Holocaust survivors].... They were very aware that the government, its agencies and Canadian employers were discriminating against Jews because they were not considered appropriate for work as loggers, farmers, miners, domestics or nurses. (51)

When Sam Bronfman and Saul Hayes [CJC] met with the Prime Minister and cabinet members in February 1947, they suggested that the needle trades had specific shortages that could be remedied by what was clearly a specifically Jewish solution. Once again, [PM William Lyon Mackenzie] King was non-committal.... Hayes [was convinced] a coordinated national strategy was necessary.... By March, Toronto, Montreal and Winnipeg were on board and a campaign to recruit participation from clothing companies across the country began. (52)

Industry leaders immediately went to work corralling employers of all faiths to produce formal requisitions for two thousand DPs.... As he was about to leave for Europe as part of the selection team, Toronto manufacturer Max Enkin wrote a personal appeal to a colleague emphasizing the humanitarian nature of the project. "We are given a great privilege of saving people" he wrote, "and I know that you would not want it on your conscience to have not participated in such a scheme." Enkin recalled that "Whatever little resistance existed was soon shamed away, however, when one firm, the principal owners of which were Gentiles, signed up for 150 workers—all of whom they could well have done without." (53)

By mid-October, 1947, the [DP selection] committee had interviewed more than a thousand displaced persons and the team expected that the first groups would be leaving for Canada by mid-November. Matthew Ram, a young Canadian social worker who had worked with the team would be left behind in Europe to keep the project on track. Ram was soon advised by the American Joint Distribution Committee (JDC) that not only were Canadian officials "very rigid" in their interpretation of the screening guidelines, they were giving precedence to the other bulk labour schemes [and not to tailors]. The JDC informed Ram that instead of the one hundred Jewish DPs expected to sail on the first ship, there would only be thirteen. When the USS *General S.D. Sturgis* left for Canada on the first day of December, there were indeed some tailors on board. Not one was Jewish. (141)

> While at a stopover in England, my father was taken aside and told there could be no more than 50 per cent Jews accepted under this program (a decision of the government). Heartbroken, they still continued. (227 [Afterword by Larry Enkin])
>
> At its completion [through to 1949] the Tailor Project had resettled some 2,500 European Jews in Canada. (225)

I leave it to you to read *The Tailor Project* and find out how Max Enkin, Saul Hayes, and the others were able to accomplish this important work while facing such fierce government obstruction.

Acknowledgements

Special thanks to my wife, Daniella Givon, for encouraging me to publish this book more than 25 years after I initially wrote it. I am grateful to my siblings, Helen and Max, for reminding or correcting me about some of the events in this book. And thank you to my children, Michael and Eitan, for their interest in their family roots.

PHOTOGRAPHS

Rachel Pinsky, circa 1941. Rubin's sister was murdered in the Holocaust at age 10.

Rubin, circa 1946.

Harry Pinsky, circa 1946.

Chasia Pinsky (later Frajdenrajch), circa 1947.

From left: *Rubin, Harry, Chasia, and Joe Frajdenrajch, 1947.*

Rubin, circa 1949.

From left: *Sam, Mendel, Fanny, and Jenny Moser, circa 1947.*

-60-

NO.	NAME	SEX	MARITAL STATUS	CHIL.	REL. & NAT.	AGE	CAMP
90	PEREJMA, Mykola	M	S	0	GC Polen	32	Landeck 1
66	PEREL, Izak	M	S	0	Jew. Pol.	25	Stuttgart 1
35	PERSINOVIC, Franjo	M	S	0	RC Yug.	34	Klagenfurt & Weidmansdorf
83	PESLA, Osip	M	S	0	GC Pol.	24	Salzburg 1
489	PETERAITIS, Oskar	M	M	1	Prot.	39	Bucholz 1
491	PETERSONAS, Juozas	M	S	0	Prot.	37	Bucholz 1
119	PETKEVICZ, Heinrichs	M	S	0	Evang. Lat.	33	Shleswig-Holstein 1
787	PETMAN, Leopold	M	S	0	Jew. Hung.	22	Bucholz 1
355	PETRASHKO, Nikolaus	M	S	0	GC Pol/Uk.	33	Munich 1
69	PETRAUSKAITE, Stefania	F	S	0	RC Lith.	35	Amberg 1
597	PETRELIS, Jonas	M	M	1	RC Lith.	45	Bucholz 1
290	PETRIW, Lydia	F	S	0	GC Pol/Uk.	24	Graz Area
742	PETRIWSKY, Pavlo	M	M	0	GC Ukr.	37	Salzburg 2
248	PETRUCHIN, Maria	F	S	0	GC Pol.	23	Landeck 2
40	PETRYNKO, Michal	M	S	0	RC Pol.	35	Shleswig-Holstein 1
492	PETUSKA, Juoszas	M	S	0	RC	37	Bucholz 1
101	PIATEK, Bronisl.	F	S	0	RC Pol.	31	Stuttgart 1
27	PIECAITIS, Petras	M	S	0	RC Lith.	32	Munich 1
179	PIEPRZ, Berek	M	M	1	Jew. Pol.	28	Frankfurt 2
32	PIERNIKOW, Sara (List 2)	F	S	0	Jew. Pol.	34	Linz Area 1
46	PIITEA, Linda	F	W	0	Evan. Est.	34	Shleswig-Holstein 2
166	PIK, Helene	M	S	0	Jew. Pol.	28	Bucholz 2
59	PIKEVICIUS, Povilas	M	M	1	RC Lith.	41	North-Rhine Westphalia 1
678	PILHUJ, Dymtro	M	M	1	GC Pol.	25	Bucholz 1
522	PINCZEWSKI, Majer	M	M	0	Jew. Pol.	37	Bucholz 1
71	PINIKAITE, Stase	F	S	0	RC Lith.	31	Amberg 1
521	PINKOS, Geniek	M	M	0	Jew. Pol.	21	Bucholz 1
228	PINSKI, Hercel	M	S	0	Jew. Pol.	27	Bucholz 1
227	PINSKI, Rubin	M	S	0	Jew. Pol.	20	Bucholz 1
133	PISAREK, Chaim	M	M	0	Jew. Pol.	35	Bucholz 1
67	PISLIAR, Anna	F	S	0	Prot. Youk.	17	Kufstein 2
828	PITKEWICZ, Feliks	M	S	0	Jew. Pol.	28	Bucholz 1
134	PLACHTA, Natan	M	M	1	Jew. Pol.	30	Bucholz 1
13	PLASECKA, Stefania	F	S	0	RC Pol.	45	Bucholz 1

A page from the ship's manifest of the USS General S.D. Sturgis, *which left Braemanhaven, Germany, on January 5, 1948, with Rubin and Harry on board.*

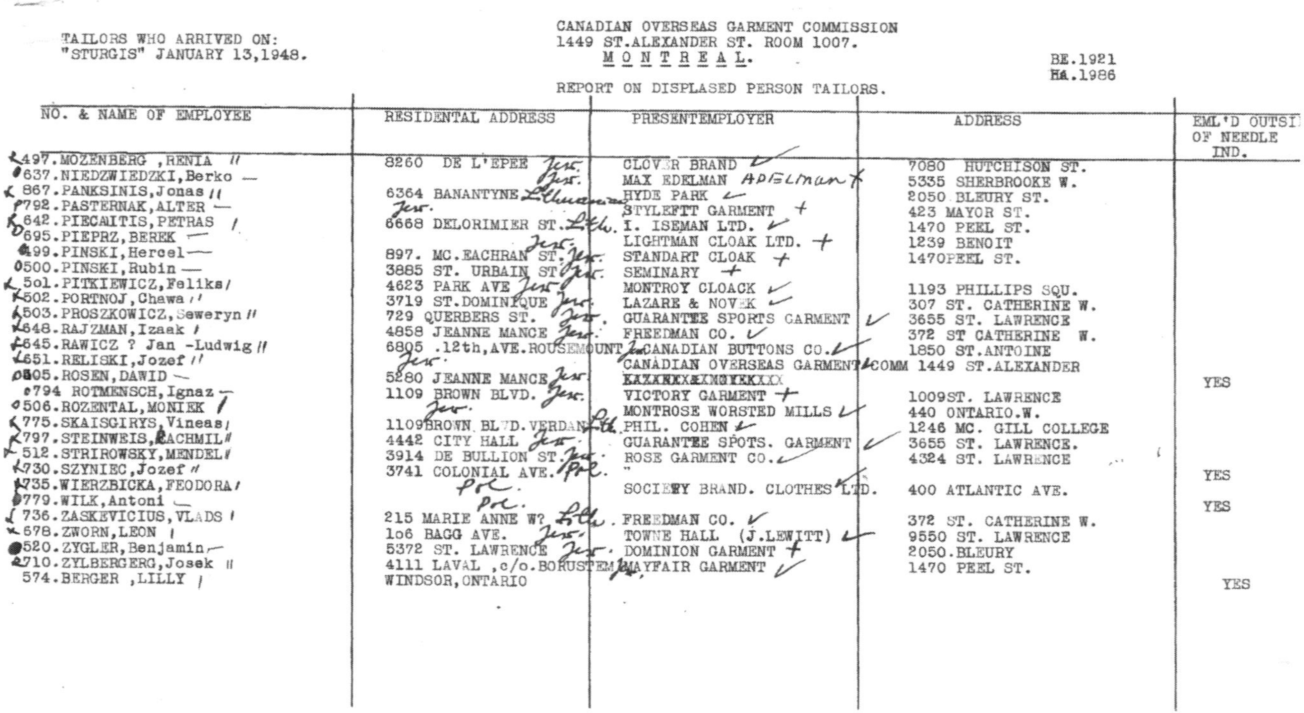

TAILORS WHO ARRIVED ON:
"STURGIS" JANUARY 13,1948.

CANADIAN OVERSEAS GARMENT COMMISSION
1449 ST.ALEXANDER ST. ROOM 1007.
M O N T R E A L.

BE.1921
HA.1986

REPORT ON DISPLASED PERSON TAILORS.

NO. & NAME OF EMPLOYEE	RESIDENTAL ADDRESS	PRESENTEMPLOYER	ADDRESS	EML'D OUTSI OF NEEDLE IND.
497.MOZENBERG ,RENIA	8260 DE L'EPEE	CLOVER BRAND	7080 HUTCHISON ST.	
637.NIEDZWIEDZKI,Berko		MAX EDELMAN	5335 SHERBROOKE W.	
867.PANKSINIS,Jonas	6364 BANANTYNE	HYDE PARK	2050 BLEURY ST.	
792.PASTERNAK,ALTER		STYLEFTT GARMENT	423 MAYOR ST.	
642.PIECAITIS,PETRAS	6668 DELORIMIER ST.	I. ISEMAN LTD.	1470 PEEL ST.	
695.PIEPRZ,BEREK		LIGHTMAN CLOAK LTD.	1239 BENOIT	
499.PINSKI,Hercel	897. MC.EACHRAN ST.	STANDART CLOAK	1470PEEL ST.	
500.PINSKI,Rubin	3885 ST. URBAIN ST	SEMINARY		
501.PITKIEWICZ,Feliks	4623 PARK AVE	MONTROY CLOACK	1193 PHILLIPS SQU.	
502.PORTNOJ,Chawa	3719 ST.DOMINIQUE	LAZARE & NOVEK	307 ST. CATHERINE W.	
503.PROSZKOWICZ,Seweryn	729 QUERBERS ST.	GUARANTEE SPORTS GARMENT	3655 ST. LAWRENCE	
648.RAJZMAN,Izaak	4858 JEANNE MANCE	FREEDMAN CO.	372 ST CATHERINE W.	
645.RAWICZ ? Jan -Ludwig	6805 .12th,AVE.ROUSEMOUNT	CANADIAN BUTTONS CO.	1850 ST.ANTOINE	
651.RELISKI,Jozef		CANADIAN OVERSEAS GARMENT COMM	1449 ST.ALEXANDER	
805.ROSEN,DAWID	5280 JEANNE MANCE	XXXXXXXXXXXXXXX		YES
794 ROTMENSCH,Ignaz	1109 BROWN BLVD.	VICTORY GARMENT	1009ST. LAWRENCE	
506.ROZENTAL,MONIEK		MONTROSE WORSTED MILLS	440 ONTARIO.W.	
775.SKAISGIRYS,Vineas	1109BROWN BLVD. VERDAN	PHIL. COHEN	1246 MC. GILL COLLEGE	
797.STEINWEIS,RACHMIL	4442 CITY HALL	GUARANTEE SPOTS. GARMENT	3655 ST. LAWRENCE.	
512.STRIROWSKY,MENDEL	3914 DE BULLION ST.	ROSE GARMENT CO.	4324 ST. LAWRENCE	
730.SZYNIEC,Jozef	3741 COLONIAL AVE.	"		
735.WIERZBICKA,FEODORA				YES
779.WILK,Antoni		SOCIETY BRAND. CLOTHES LTD.	400 ATLANTIC AVE.	YES
736.ZASKEVICIUS,VLADS	215 MARIE ANNE W?	FREEDMAN CO.	372 ST. CATHERINE W.	
678.ZWORN,LEON	1o6 BAGG AVE.	TOWNE HALL (J.LEWITT)	9550 ST. LAWRENCE	
520.ZYGLER,Benjamin	5372 ST. LAWRENCE	DOMINION GARMENT	2050.BLEURY	
710.ZYLBERGERG,Josek	4111 LAVAL ,c/o.BORUSTEM	MAYFAIR GARMENT	1470 PEEL ST.	
574.BERGER ,LILLY	WINDSOR,ONTARIO			YES

A page from the Canadian Overseas Garment Commission's "Report on Displaced Person Tailors," which lists employment of tailors who arrived on the USS General S.D. Sturgis *on January 13, 1948, including Rubin and Harry Pinsky.*

Rubin and Jenny, March 18, 1951.

From left: *Sam, Jenny, Fanny, and Mendel Moser, Harry Pinsky, and baby Helen Pinsky, 1952.*

From left: *Pola Brzezinski (née Krolewicki) and her daughter Esther, Rubin, and Chasia Frajdenrajch, 1961.*

Rubin and Jenny in Hawaii, 1970.

Rubin and Jenny at home in Regina, 1973.

Second row, left to right: *Jenny, Rubin, and Helen;* first row, left to right: *Bernard, his wife Daniella Givon, and Max Pinsky, 1979.*

Fourth row, left to right: *Leona, Simon and Max Pinsky, Helen Pinsky and husband Victor Elias, Bernard Pinsky and wife Daniella Givon;* third row, left to right: *Isaac Elias, Rubin, Jenny, Michael Pinsky;* second row, left to right: *Ben Elias, Eitan Pinsky;* first row, left to right: *Jacob Elias, Rachael Pinsky, 1993. This includes all Rubin and Jenny's grandchildren except Tova and Rina, born later.*

Jenny, Max's wife Leona Pinsky, and Chasia Frajdenrajch, 1996.

Rubin and Jenny, 1996.

Manufactured by Amazon.ca
Acheson, AB

14275034R00125